THE HEALING PATHS OF FIFE

A Fantasy - Memoir
Diana's Walk along the
Fife Coastal Path

By
Diana Jackson

Diana Jackson © Copyright 2017

The right of Diana Jackson to be identified as author of this
work has been asserted by her in accordance with the Copyright,
Designs and Patents Act 1988.

All Rights Reserved

No reproduction, copy or transmission of this publication may
be made without written permission. No paragraph of this
publication may be reproduced, copied or transmitted save with the
written permission of the author, or in accordance with the
provisions of the Copyright Act 1956 (as amended).

Any person who commits any unauthorised act in relation to
this publication may be liable to criminal prosecution and civil
claims for damages.

As Diana 'met' many people on her coastal path walk, both real
and fictitious, she tried to capture the essence of each character to
bring them back to life.

A CIP catalogue record for this title is
available from the British Library.

Softcover: ISBN:9780993260810

Part 1 published by Eventispress in 2015
The Healing Paths of Fife published by Eventispress in 2017

PART 1

From Redundancy to Rejuvenation

by

Diana Jackson

"A blend of reality and fantasy. Diana Jackson leaves it to you, the reader, to distinguish which is which."

DEDICATION

To Alex and Moira at the Wee Shoppe and our new
neighbours and friends.

CHAPTER 1

Redundancy and Opportunity

The End and the Beginning

Ode to Redundancy

Thrown on the scrap heap of time
Cull of the over 50's, teaching since the eighties
Pointless, useless, devoid of purpose.
Emptiness -
Will it ever pass?
Opportunity, change, serendipity shines.
Finding the heart of my very self,
No longer left on the dusty shelf.
Nervous, risky, exciting, new.
Fulfilling
A relief at last.

I AM TOLD that I live in a world of fantasy. Must be difficult to live with - wondering what's behind that dreamy expression,

'Anyone home?' friends would ask smiling at me,

'Did you hear a word I said,' is a common phrase my husband uses, but apart from a few 'out-of-this-world' experiences when I was younger, I think I'm quite normal. You know the sort of thing; dreams which uncannily came true; warning voices in my head which saved my life; my dead granddad visiting me when I stayed in his room after he'd died; normal stuff like that.

I thought I was pretty ordinary until the summer of 2013 that is, when we moved to Fife. Not only did we have some heart warming encounters, but some weird ones too, and I'm not quite sure that you will believe me when I tell you, but this is my story:

'I'd rather wear a rucksack on my back than a handbag on my shoulder!'

or

'A Writer's Fantasy Life in Fife'

or

'From Redundancy to Rejuvenation'

Firstly, **who am I**? I am 55 years old and wearing well I'm told. I am five foot nine I believe, unless I've shrunk with age - the little plumpness that I battle with constantly is disguised well by my height. My long naturally coloured chestnut hair, frames a relatively line free face. I always intended to have my locks cut off at 40, but then I began travelling globally and long hair fitted into my bohemian life style. Since then I have never had the courage for change, and will wait until my patient hairdresser warns me that the time has finally come to acquire a more mature image, fitting for a lady of my age. This will happen sooner rather than later I should think.

As far as to **what** I do, well, I can't answer that one right now. That's half of the problem. What I can say is who I was, and then unfold the story of how, in a supernatural sort of way, I discovered who I am now. Here goes ...

In short I had been a teacher virtually all of my working life, and for the last twelve years, until last July, I was a tutor of sixteen to nineteen year olds in a college of which I was once so proud. That was until I was given a letter offering me voluntary redundancy.

Like every other member of the teaching staff I was stunned, but after work I was heading straight to the airport to fly to Edinburgh. My husband, a kind unassuming man most of the time, was closer to retirement age than I and had been working in Scotland for several months. He had been commuting home at weekends, so we'd already planned this trip. In the last couple of weeks he had been given an option to temporarily relocate his work to Fife, and was keen to do so if I agreed, and so we had arranged that I would fly north that weekend to explore and decide together whether the move was viable. I'd already asked my line manager if a sabbatical was possible, but the letter I held tightly in my hand seemed like a gift; a nudge to say,

'Go for it. You're doing the right thing.'

So, whilst colleagues filled their time with application forms and interviews, my summer was for planning and sorting out our lives for a dramatic and life-changing experience. I like to think that serendipity shone down upon us. In many ways I was secretly relieved to be escaping to a totally different environment. I knew that I would find September a challenge emotionally, the start of a new college year, and the world I had been cleaved from. I would try to think of it like a holiday from which I did not return.

A retreat? Yes, that's what I would call it. That is, until strange things began to happen.

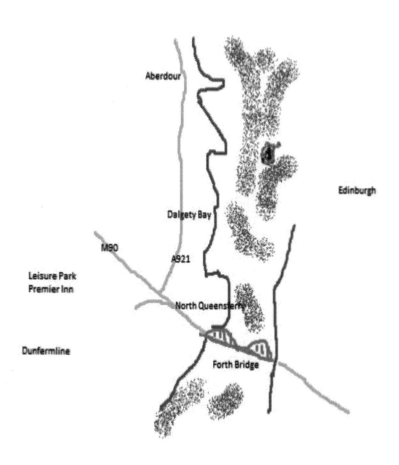

CHAPTER 2

Dunfermline

It's My Secret

WHEN WE FIRST moved up to Dunfermline the company put us up in a Premier Inn on a large entertainments park north of Edinburgh. It was a surreal existence. Don't get me wrong. The room was clean, staff friendly and more than helpful; it's just that it felt so empty. Our nearest neighbour was McDonald's and I could see a bowling alley, bingo hall and gym, not forgetting Frankie and Bennie's from our bedroom window. Very strange. This was to be our temporary home for a few weeks.

All those clichés came from people with whom we'd shared our secret.

'It will be an adventure.'

'It was meant to be.'

'These things happen for a reason.'

With all of this buzzing through my head why did I feel so vacant? In empathy with our house down south maybe. Life had seeped out of me and no one was home; less than usual anyway.

There was a lady searching for a more permanent home for us so what could I do with my time? Secretly I think she was a little exasperated because she had been enthusiastic to show my husband half a dozen flats so far, but he'd turned them all down.

Have you ever scrutinised a print on the wall of a Premier Inn. They all seem to be the same; two stalks of lavender in calming shades of purple, softened to a blurred background of violets, purples, creams and soft green. I think I could do one myself if I put my mind to it, but where was I?

Who am I? My mind drifted in a field of thoughts and lavender.

I am a redundant teacher. Thrown away. No longer required. Superfluous. Do I ever want to teach again? Would it be a shame to waste all those years of experience and enthusiasm? Do I really want to go back to that type of life? It's not the teaching that discourages me, or the students, or even my colleagues, who were truly special. No. I've been worn right down like a well used pencil by three P's; *politics*, *paperwork* and the forever having to jump through new hoops to *prove* myself. Yes *prove* myself is the third p, that anyone in the public sector of health or education will understand. It doesn't matter how many times you get a grade one or two in a dreaded Ofsted inspection, the amount of stress just increases as goal posts move or change beyond recognition.

I'm also early retired. Didn't I tell you that before? Since I'd reached 55 this summer I was able to draw on a very small pension. I may be one of the last teachers to do so early, but it eased the financial worry of my situation.

What else am I?

I stared at the lavender and took a deep breath. My pulse rate lowered.

I am a *writer* of course and have been for over ten years. For the first few years I juggled with a full time teaching post and then reduced my hours to three days per week. Now I have all the time in the world until my redundancy money runs out (or the royalties pour in!)

I had so many tasks I could focus on in that bare room. (except the lavender) There was proof reading my latest manuscript, planning a major on-line promotion campaign in the autumn for my second novel and tinkering with a few projects along the way. Not to mention beginning the serious research for the next novel in my series.

A *writer's retreat*? That's what I'm going to have – a year's sabbatical to write. How lucky is that? Or does luck really come into it?

I could be a tourist too and visit all the attractions, but now I've got to count the pennies.

Mind you, a writer is never really bored. Too many words and ideas buzzing and all it takes is a comment made, a meaningful look or noticing something a little bit odd to set the mind racing. Two people meeting furtively in a hotel car-park; colleagues or lovers? A man in well worn jacket walking into McDonald's with a little boy's hand in his, equally unkempt but at peace with the world, both faces a picture of excitement. A middle aged lady sitting on her own at a cafe in Dobbies Garden Centre, drinking coffee after coffee, just like me. What's her story?

Even so I still felt dislocated, living in a room not conducive to creativity, so what could I do about it?

In the end I jotted any ideas down and bided my time. That was until two things happened. Firstly my husband bought me a second hand camera and secondly I made my first trip into Dunfermline and those events literally changed my life.

It was the morning after our arrival when I grabbed my 'new to me' camera and headed into the nearest shopping centre with the task of buying bedding and other items we would need for our alternative life here in Scotland. I liked Dunfermline instantly; it had character and history and the main street buzzed with life. A good sign. After a while I remembered seeing St Margaret's Cave mentioned so sneaked a peep at my map, then I headed in what looked like the right direction.

With the bus station on my right and a bit of a tired end of Dunfermline in front of me, a back street with empty shop fronts a plenty, I was led to steep steps with a sign to the caves. Intrigued, I followed them down to a car park. There I felt compelled to take my first photo, at which point the tarmac disappeared, replaced by a wooded glen with a narrow path leading to a cave.

At the entrance a nun handed me a lighted candle, a spare candle and a kindling box and undeterred I headed into the gloom, the shadows of light flickering on the uneven walls and crevices. At its extremity there was a grotto, the rock-face naturally arching above a simple altar on which was a bronze cross and beside it a plain wooden bench for prayer. I tilted my candle to allow some wax to drip on a shelf already covered with tell-tale hardened globules and pushed it firmly in place, forming a circlet of light.

I knelt down and waited.

Silence.

'Where do I go from here?' I whispered.

Silence.

'I need to know.' my words barely audible this time.

Quiet. Peace.

I must have remained there many moments before asking with an urgency which echoed back along the cave,

'Please, can you tell me who I am?'

'Yes, I can,' said a crisp clear voice to my left, 'but are you ready to listen?'

'I am,' I replied, this time with more conviction.

The lady standing before me wore in a long brown robe, much like the nun who had shown me the way in, and yet here was an imposing woman whose presence filled the room with a unique combination of authority and humility; her features, beneath her hood, serene and virtually flawless.

'What do you want to know, my daughter?' she asked kindly.

'I'm not really sure,' but then I told her my story. She listened, her eyes focussed on my face and ever-changing expressions.

'I believe that you are at the start of a very special stage of your life. This will be overflowing with blessings and yet there will be sacrifices to be made too. At first it will be a secret time - a time of journey, a time of discovery and you will long to shout about it to the world, but you must not do so until the time is right. You must promise me that.' She waited. I was speechless so she continued.

'So, my advice is this, that you go forth, and on your way you will learn to value who you are and discover who you might be. You will, I hope, let go of all that is drawing you back in the past and embrace what the future holds for you.'

'But where should I go?'

'There's an abundance of beautiful places along our coastal waters of the Firth of Forth here in Fife, with mysteries you shall uncover, and very soon you shall find a village where you will be welcomed and will truly feel at home.'

'How will I know?'

'You **will** know; that is all I can say, if you let it be as it should be. Come,' she said.

I followed the lady out of the cave and to the top of a hill where we looked down over the river.

'Yonder is the ferry which I established for pilgrims on their journey from Dunfermline to St Andrews. Think of your life akin to theirs; seeking peace but also filling with much joy.'

The lady's expression was enveloped by an overwhelming sadness as she continued. 'Whereas I am certain that when I next take the ferry over to Edinburgh, I face great suffering from whence I will never return.' She paused, taking a deep breath before adding, 'Be thankful for who you are my daughter.' then she held out her hands cupping my own, her eyes compassionate with a hint of the grief that she alluded to. As she gestured for me to return to the cave alone I wondered who she was, but when I turned to express my thanks she had vanished and behind me was a long tunnel, lit by low level electric lights - the candles gone.

I glanced over my shoulder and filled my head with the prayer,

'Please help me to find out who I am. Give me the strength to make sacrifices when the time comes and to be sure of your will in my life.' I am not sure to whom I prayed; the strange lady or to God. It didn't seem to matter. It had certainly been a very long time since I had prayed like that. The words were unfamiliar to me and yet warming. Talking of warmth I suddenly felt a chill and so I walked along the tunnel, ever upwards. Occasionally, I could not resist to pause and read the various boards about St Margaret, who I now believed had been talking to me a few moment ago.

At the cave entrance was a soberly dressed mature but kindly lady, who looked up at me in surprise.

'I didn't see you go in,' she said. 'Please can you sign the visitors' book before you leave.'

'An unforgettable experience,' I wrote under comments next to my name. 'The start of many,' I added before emerging at the edge of the car park which I had looked down upon earlier in the day.

That night I recorded St Margaret's story in my notebook:

Queen Margaret was the second wife of Malcolm Canmore, Malcolm lll of Scotland who was king in the early 11th century. A pious lady and devout Catholic, by example she fed the poor and guided her courtiers to change their ways - the men to be more courteous and civilised and the ladies to be pure and devout. Although she had churches built, it was to a cave that she liked to go for her personal devotions. A ferry across The

Firth of Forth from Queensferry to North Queensferry was attributed to Margaret, to carry pilgrims. She returned to Edinburgh when she heard that her husband and son Edward had been *slain in the Battle of Alnwick and sadly Margaret died not long after.*

Now I knew where I should go to next.

CHAPTER 3

Kinghorn and Pettycur

We Found Kinghorn ~or Did Kinghorn Find Us?

I WALKED BACK up the town and into the Dunfermline tourist information centre and browsed the walking section. 'Fife Coastal Path' leapt out at me, not literally but you know how it is when a cover grabs your attention. This was a detailed map of the Fife coast, places I might visit and what I might see along the way. I love to walk and better still it doesn't cost a lot; just the odd cup of tea here and there.

That evening we drove along to a small Victorian resort called Burntisland, that's *Burnt...island* and not *Burnt...is...land!*, and we ate fish and chips out of the wrapper, sitting by the shore. At one point I looked up eastwards along the bay.

'Could we drive a couple of miles along the coast to a little place called Kinghorn before going back to the hotel?' I asked my husband Richard.

'Yes, I should think so.'

I paused.

'It's just that I saw an attractive flat to rent on the Internet and the place looked quite pretty; like Cornwall and the

Channel Islands rolled into one,' I answered the unspoken 'why' in his voice. You see my husband had always dreamed of living in Cornwall and I, on Alderney. Each year our holidays took us to either the island of my dreams and my family roots or to the West Country, a place with so many family memories for Richard.

He agreed to pander to my whim and so we parked above the small harbour and bay, reminiscent of the west coast of England. At once I felt an enormous peace. All the waiting and wondering of the last few months settled in that moment.

'I could feel at home here,' I said.

'It's lovely isn't it,' my husband replied.

The following morning the lady, who was taking us to see some property, apologised that the flat I had mentioned had been taken, 'but,' she added, seeing my forlorn expression in her car mirror, 'both places I'm showing you today are in Kinghorn, too.'

I cheered instantly.

The first was unfurnished and therefore unsuitable, but then we drove down Pettycur Road to Pettycur Bay and, passing the wee fishing harbour on our left, we were faced by a sweeping sandy bay with traditional green caravans dotted on the cliff face ahead of us. Delightful.

We were shown up to the third floor of a small block of flats - the top floor in fact.

'That's stunning,' I said as I gazed out of the window over the sands.

'We'll take it,' my husband said, even before we'd seen the rest of the flat.

When we got back to the purple walls of our hotel room we could not even remember if there had been a TV or a table. All we could remember was that it was clean, had two bedrooms and that wonderful view!

It was a nail biting time over the following Bank Holiday weekend until the property agents confirmed that we had been accepted and had cleared all their checks. That was truly a moment of celebration so we headed for the Italian Restaurant on the Leisure Complex, not exciting I know, but our life in Fife had truly begun.

It was another two weeks before we would move in at the beginning of September, a perfect time for me to buy all the things we needed and look forward to our future, but it was also time for my journey of discovery to begin in earnest.

Ode to Kinghorn
You stole my heart
the moment we met
as I gazed down from the Braes.
The warm sun
captured in the palm of your hand
even on the coldest winter morning.
The amphitheatre of
Victorian elegance and fishermen's cottages mingling,
reflecting that warmth.
The unforgettable welcome of the Wee Shoppe
where gossip's shared and friendships forged.
Oh Kinghorn! How I thank you
for taking us in and giving us a home.

CHAPTER 4

North Queensferry and The Forth Railbridge

Strive For Excellence in Everything

THE FOLLOWING DAY I headed towards the iconic Forth bridges and parked almost under the railway bridge at North Queensferry, only a couple of miles from Dunfermline. In my reverie I imagined Queen Margaret welcoming pilgrims from their long and arduous trips. Today I was mesmerised by the imposing structure before me; a container ship sliding smoothly under a burnt orange iron arch, narrowly missing the little fortified island of Inchgarvie. I took a picture capturing the moment and was relieved to check that all was well. The image was true to life; not tampered with.

Stretching my legs I walked around the relatively unspoilt village with its small ferry service for tourists - a remnant of its importance in days long past. I lifted my camera towards the blue and white *Forth Belle,* immediately checking the shot, but this time the camera revealed a man with a distinctive bowler hat who was alighting a black and white funnelled vessel; the master peering irritably from under his cap as he kept his vessel steady for his mate to leap off and secure the ropes. I smiled. The man in the bowler was too impatient to wait for the protocol of the captain's say so that all was safe to disembark. To my dismay this arrogant man was heading straight towards me.

'Move out of the way,' the distinguished gentleman shouted. 'This is no place for a lady. Don't you know that there are more accidents caused by people gawping under structures such as this, than skilled men falling off them!'

I looked up and to my amazement the bridge was no longer a solid structure all the way towards the Edinburgh coast but one piece was missing, the section before the last pillar. I glanced further down the river and my fears were confirmed. The road bridge had disappeared too.

'Come,' he shouted, as if barking orders to one of his men, 'join me for refreshments.' He paused, suddenly aware of what appeared to him to be my strange attire. 'If you will,' he added with almost a smile. I followed the man up the slope towards the Albert Hotel where he held the door for me to step inside.

'John Fowler at your service Madam,' he said as he gestured for me to sit at a small round table near to the door. I could sense the pointed stares from the bar as we settled down while tea was brought to us. He nodded for me to pour, but gave me little time to dwell on the absurdity of my situation - just enough to calculate that I must have time travelled back over 120 years.

With no preamble he began with a direct question, which was more of an order.

'Tell me who you are and what you do,' he said.

I gulped, as if this was the most important interview of my life.

'I'm a writer,' spilled from my lips, 'and my name is Diana Jackson.'

'Good good. That wasn't so hard was it? Why are you so afraid of your gift? Why do you hide behind it, make excuses about it and regret that other tag to your identity?' without waiting for a reply he continued. 'Now say it again, only this time with conviction.'

'My name is Diana Jackson and I am a writer,' I said, my eyes bright and my chin held high.

'That's more like it lass,' he replied in his broad Yorkshire accent.

'Now, I only have a short time with you but I do have a message and a wealth of experience in my field of engineering. I've lived a long life and achieved great things. Whether I'm designing bridges, a cartographer in Egypt, deer stalking in my favourite Braemar or yachting in Dorset, do I ever sit back and wonder who I am? No!' and he slammed his china tea cup down in the saucer making the tea spill over.

'No,' he said more gently. 'I live each day as if it is my last and every moment I give of my best. Each project I undertake has to be perfectly designed and skilfully executed. It's my job to see to that.'

'I understand,' I said, thinking of everything this famous man had achieved in his life.

'So why are you dithering? Why do you waste so much time? Write, write, write and with each word improve your skills. Ask yourself, is that particular word perfect for the task or should I choose another? Check and double check. Revise, amend and if it's not perfect start again.' He gulped down the last dregs of his tea and I was amused when he scowled as tea leaves caught in his mouth. He was at least human.

24

'Come,' he said, 'you may follow my morning and write about me as you asked in your letter, but every word must count. I'm an engineer. What would happen if my measurements were not precise?'

I had little time to wonder what he meant by a letter - a case of mistaken identity maybe.

As we left the hotel he pointed skywards. 'Look up at that girder hovering in the sky. How would I look if it was even a pin head short?' He paused again but didn't wait. I didn't dare reply. ' A fool,' he boomed, and the people around looked at me knowingly, but I tried not to cower. 'I won't have time to speak with you again but here's my gift of time to you. Use it wisely.'

I observed Sir John Fowler for the remainder of morning - the way he spoke with firmness and was held with respect by all around him. There was a moment when all was still - his hand almost glued to his forehead. The girder hovered. Everyone gasped. It was lowered slowly, ever so slowly into place. A perfect fit. When Sir John looked back over his shoulder, did he wink at me or was all of this in my imagination?

Seconds later I was aware of the seagulls yet again and the waters lapping at the quay. I retrieved my notepad and started to write:

March 1890

'Today is the historic moment when the banks of the Firth of Forth have been coupled. Sir John Fowler's latest design of a rail track which will span the waters linking north and south,

Edinburgh with Perth, the lowlands with the highlands, has been accomplished. Standing here beside the looming arches on the North Queensferry bank I can see the Mayor of Edinburgh and his entourage on the far shore waiting, all gazing upwards at this awe inspiring sight. In unison we held our breath as Fowler's precision engineering skills are put to the test. A lone piper plays. A gasp rings out as the last girder is lowered perfectly and precisely in place. A cheer rose from both sides of the water and a brass band added to the cacophony of sound.'

I turned and strolled up through the village towards my first stretch of the Fife Coastal Path above North Queensferry, clearly signposted - only pausing to sit on a bench looking out towards the bridges. A cruise ship *The Queen Elizabeth* had come into view. What a magnificent sight! Three feats of engineering, the ship beside the rail bridge where it moored to give its passengers access to Edinburgh, and the more modern road bridge behind.

As I glanced down, the *Forth Belle* chugged its way back across the river, and time seemed to stand still. It was as if 900 years had been bridged - both Margaret and John Fowler achieving greatness. It was fitting that my journey should begin here but as I walked a little further around the cliff top walk I could see the Fife Coast ahead of me and my days to come.

A couple stopped to talk. 'We moved here ten years ago,' the lady said.

'Wouldn't live anywhere else,' the man added. 'Fife seems to have its own micro climate.'

'I can quite believe it,' I replied, shading my eyes from the sunshine.

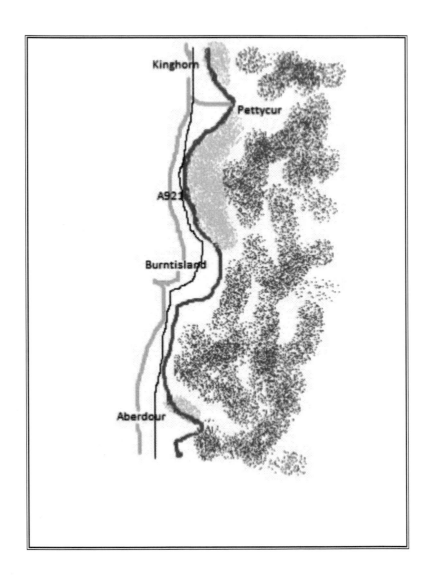

CHAPTER 5

Aberdour

Once a Teacher Always a Teacher

THE FOLLOWING MONDAY was a personal red letter day, the seventh day since I had left home in Bedfordshire and the day my colleagues, those fortunate (though a matter of opinion) to keep their jobs, returned to their 'new look' college. They say that the beginning of the new academic year is the hardest time for any retiring teacher, whose vocation has been a substantial part of life for over 30 years.

I explored my feelings. Was I smug or just a touch jealous of those experiencing some kind of normality. My mind drifted. How would life be if I was one of them? Nervous, resigned, shaking myself after a restless night. What would have made it just a tad more bearable? I sighed. The pleasures, stresses, satisfaction, pain and sheer joy teaching brought over the years has helped to mould me into the person that I am. I must be grateful for that.

I used the Sat Nav to find a launderette but once my chores were out of the way I headed back to the coast and was drawn to a little place called Aberdour, a town with a castle, gift shops and a sign to say that it had won a Gold Award for

Beautiful Fife in 2013. (Each year to date I believe) I wanted to send a postcard so I popped into the post office.

'There they are,' replied the kindly post office man. 'There's a funny story to tell about them,' he said as I began to write my card.

'When my wife and I first moved here the postcards were all of another generation entirely so one of my first tasks was to up-date them. I found a company on the Internet and sent them an email. They replied that all I would have to do was to send them good quality digital photos and it would be no problem. Where are you based? I asked in my next message. We're in Burntisland, they said. I couldn't believe it. They were only three miles up the road from us and so offered to come to take the photos for us!'

I laughed and picked out a postcard of a sensory garden. 'Where's this?' I asked.

'Carry on up the road towards the railway station and you will see it opposite.'

I thanked him and went on my way. I smiled as I walked along the main street towards the station. This was the first of many tales the Post Office man would share with me during our stay in Fife.

(The man in the Post Office has now retired and the shop has been turned into a Deli by two enterprising ladies now so I'm told, but they still offer Post Office services)

A waft of lavender greeted me as I walked through the arch, reminding me of our temporary home. Closing my eyes a moment, intensifying my sense of smell, I breathed deeply. Walking on I was aware of the changing textures underfoot;

gravel, wood, sand and stone, all making imprints on the soles of my feet - unique sounds with each step. I brushed sensuous grasses with the palm of my hand, stopping to admire a crab apple tree in glorious isolation, the tiny fruit perfectly formed, lighting up a niche of the garden. Although close to a main road the world seemed lost to me. The metal seals, the sedum and a sea of perennial geraniums led me to a plaque on the wall informing me that that I was standing on the location of the old school house, pulled down and derelict for a while before the area was beautifully landscaped. I turned, took a photo and was instantly aware of echoes of juggling crockery in the school canteen and children's laughter as a train rumbled by.

I knelt down next to one group of youngsters and, noticing their unfashionable dress I realised that I was gazing at children much like myself at primary school back in the 1960's.

'Who are you?' asked a young girl with a cheeky grin and, of course, that soft lilt which spoke of Scotland rather than the Home Counties where I grew up.

'I was once a teacher,' I said, 'but now I'm a writer.'

'I write stories; fairy stories and tales about the sea, when sea creatures talk to me,' she said.

'That's lovely. I hope you keep them safe and illustrate them.'

'Oh, I could do, couldn't I; I could buy a little exercise book and keep them altogether. That's a great idea. I will!'

I had no time to answer this young authoress, whose enthusiasm would drive her on, because an imposing man in a suit tapped me on the shoulder.

'I apologize for the noise. I'm Mr Davids the headmaster. Everyone calls me Pop.' He paused, scrutinising my appearance, but he must have thought me harmless because he smiled before continuing, 'and who might you be?'

'I'm Diana Jackson and...,' I swallowed.

'You were once a teacher but now you're a writer. Yes, I overheard. It's as if you've practised the speech but don't quite believe it yet.' He gazed thoughtfully at me, not in an unpleasant way. 'Come into my office,' he said.

I had no time to wonder what or how. I also recognised the voice of authority so I smiled back at the little girl and followed Mr Davids, a tall man with round spectacles, who strode away with me rushing in his wake.

'I understand that you are not seeking a new position,' he said. 'In fact I cannot offer you one. We're about to move to new buildings and this school will be demolished.'

He stopped to peer at me through spectacled eyes. I almost cowered in the face of authority, like a child again. After all, I had no right to be there.

'You will always be a teacher,' he continued, 'Keep your eyes open for opportunities to share wisdom and they will come to you in the most unexpected ways. Never feel that your skills are wasted, just transferable.' He smiled for the first time.

It was a phrase I had used in abundance with my students. If they were in a football team they were good team players. If they made their own clothes they paid attention to detail and could follow both written and pictorial instructions. If they played pool then they had good spatial awareness and a realisation that they needed to apply just the right amount of pressure to be successful. All those skills were transferable.

'I understand,' I said.

'In some ways I can see that you grieve a lack of purpose in your life. Don't. Let go and learn from your own sound advice, but keep an eye open for new directions and ideas.'

As I shook Mr Davids' hand and left the building I noticed that I was heading toward the archway and could smell the lavender again. The school had vanished.

I continued my walk, passing the railway station and taking the footpath along the edge of the track until eventually, after crossing the road beside the modern school, I came to an open field leading down to a bay which I knew to have the delightful name of Silver Sands. I had a Panini in the cafe beside the beach, which became one of our favourite haunts in the months to come, before continuing towards the lighthouse. The path was in shadow at first so the contrast of light as I walked over the rocky ridge was breathtaking as I gazed along the coast and back towards The Forth Bridges. I sat for a while before taking the path across the headland and down the rugged steps towards Black Sands Bay and the sheltered harbour of sailing yachts.

Back at the hotel that night I reflected on my day, recording the following account of the old school at Aberdour in my notebook:

Train Disruption Causes School Closure in 1967
The old school at Aberdour has now closed, mainly due to the interruption of noise and vibration from the trains adjacent

to the building. It will shortly be demolished and the children moved to new premises on Hawkcraig Road. Headmaster Mr Davids, locally known as Pop, said that a new era will be good for the school and village but that consideration needed to be made as to what to do with the abandoned site, it being strategically placed in the heart of the village across the road from the railway station.

It was the last night of The Edinburgh Festival so that evening we decided to seize the moment and head for St David's Harbour, part of Dalgety Bay, between North Queensferry and Aberdour. It was almost directly across the Forth to Edinburgh, so we waited expectantly as the sun set. I suggested we try to find Forth FM and within moments we were tuned into the 'live' music from the celebrations' final moments. Then we sat mesmerised as closely choreographed fireworks lit the sky. It seemed to us a sign of positive endings and a promise for a new beginning.

CHAPTER 6

Aberdour to Burntisland ~ and Kinghorn

Water is the Food of Life

SITTING IN OUR purple surroundings the next day I was filled with irrational thoughts, verging on despair; by no means the tranquillity intended. A sense of loss and fear of the unknown fought for my attention. I knew that fresh air, exercise and glorious scenery would enhance my perspective and so I headed back to Aberdour to continue the walk to Burntisland. The path is betwixt the railway line and the rugged water's edge where, at times, seals are seen swimming, then it veers under a short tunnel and through to a woodland walk on the other side of the track. Very soon I spotted the legendary waterfall and stood for a few moments watching the waters cascade down the rocks. I had read that, if you leave a coin in the pools of water it will turn green - such is the effect of minerals flowing from the rocks above. I dropped a 10p coin in for luck and stood back to take a photo. I glanced about me, teasing myself that a Selkie might appear - a mythical creature who is able to shed its seal skin to become human, often with dire consequences. They are said to be quite handsome with seductive and destructive powers. As that moment two walkers came by and one of the ladies pointed further down the path.

'There always used to be a metal cup attached to the rocks by a chain nearby,' one of the ladies said. 'I think it was put there for the soldiers passing through in the war.'

'That's interesting,' I said as she smiled and they continued on their way. I wished I had asked her which war it was. I reached for my camera and, as I turned, not just one but a troop of men appeared along the path. They marched passed me towards the tunnel in their clean khaki uniforms and peaked caps, which barely hid their smiles. Many stopped to take hold of a cup which before that moment had remained hidden. Several paused to fill it with water from the burn and, once refreshed, quickened their pace to get in step with the others once more. Only one man stopped to look at me and he was obviously in charge of the men. He offered me the cup which I felt compelled to take.

'Man can live without food for a while but not without water and you canna better spring water, pure and simple,' he said as I returned the cup to him from which he drank eagerly. He bowed, a small imperceptible nod of the head before rushing to rejoin his men. When I looked down only the ring remained where the cup had been. I hadn't even identified which soldiers they were, and the encounter had been too brief to enquire. World War One I guessed, maybe naval men waiting to set sail in one of the ships moored nearby; the path being the shortest distance between harbours. I made a note to research it if I could and continued to walk.

As I entered Burntisland I passed some interesting buildings which spoke of past wealth; the first of note was

Rossend Castle, a favourite haunt of Mary Queen of Scots and other monarchs, so the history books tell us. Near the station was Somerville Square, dwellings for 16th and 17th Century merchants including Mary Somerville. Now there's a person I would have liked to meet. I read that she was a 19th Century mathematician and astronomer. I took a photo and looked around but was disappointed that no one appeared.

Nearby was a second-hand bookshop, an Aladdin's Cave of tomes, ancient and relatively modern, where I could have spent hours, as well as pounds. On the advice of the keeper of this wonderful place, who assured me that the author was a local man, I left with a copy of *'The Fife Coast'* by Hamish Brown under my arm. On leaving I remembered the cup near the waterfall, or the lack of it.

'Ah, I know,' he said. 'It was still there until a few years ago. Health and safety probably. Anyway, as far as I know it was for any traveller on their way along the coast, since it used to be the main thoroughfare before the road was built.'

'Thank you,' I said and left, realising how easy it is for stories to be passed and altered by hearsay, and wondering, not for the first time, how we know that any written history is accurate. It's a conundrum. Nevertheless I felt reassured that naval personnel would almost certainly have walked that route too and so was content with the works of my imagination.

Wandering along the main street of Burntisland I noticed a fresh-fishmongers, butchers and greengrocers - shops to explore later, and with the words of the soldier echoing in my mind I vowed to buy local fresh food as much as I could in future months. After treating myself to a cup of tea in a little cafe, where children were decorating their own plates ready for firing, I retraced my steps to the station and caught the train back to Aberdour. Whilst waiting for the train I read the interesting fact that Burntisland was once the first ever rail ferry in the UK. I couldn't help but wonder if a ferry, which would only take a few minutes to Edinburgh, could be viable for commuters today.

The following Saturday I had noticed in the local press that Kinghorn were holding their autumn fair. I thought it would be fun to go and it was delightful. Having paid our entrance fee at the door of the church hall, we squeezed our way through the displays of foot long carrots and enormous onions. It was a light hearted affair with many watching the photos of the village scarecrows, which had recently appeared in various disguises all over the village, from Red Riding Hood to mermaids, causing hilarity to everyone as they walked by. As our first introduction to life in Kinghorn, this was an occasion to remember, full of cheerful enthusiasm.

On returning to the car-park I remarked,

'Look Richard, there are tables out there down in the harbour. Let's investigate.'

We took the steep steps winding down to the Lifeboat Station, an area we later discovered was known locally as The Braes, and discovered The Wee Shoppe. This harbour cafe became our most regular haunt. Frequently we paused to enjoy a cup of tea and toastie whilst breathing in the view, sheltered by the sweeping arc of Kinghorn Bay. It is a place which can be uncannily mild too, a sun-trap even in the depths of winter, where an al-fresco wee blether is even possible in January. We know because we've done it! It was at the Wee Shoppe that I first experienced first-hand the warm welcome of the people of Kinghorn. As we were leaving I happened to notice a lady sitting on her own reading. I've no idea what made me ask and Richard says I'm obsessed with recycling, but I enquired,

'I hope you don't mind me disturbing you but are you local?'

'Yes, she said in a pleasant Scottish accent. 'I live just along there.' She pointed to the stone facade of flats further along the harbour.

'It's just that we are moving in down at Pettycur on Monday and seeing all your coloured bins over there, I was wondering when the bin days are.'

The lady, who was soon to become a very dear friend, grinned at me. My husband raised his eyebrows at her.

'Well,' she said, 'I'd better not say because it's probably different down at Pettycur.'

To my relief she wasn't put off by my peculiar opening question because then she asked me,

'If you're moving in on Monday then why don't you pop down here on Tuesday morning and I'll tell you all about Kinghorn?'

'That would be lovely,' I beamed as we went on our way.

The following Tuesday I enjoyed a cuppa with the lady I had spoken to and her friend and by the time I left them I was dizzy with so many suggestions of groups to join and events to participate in.

Thus I'd made contact with local people even before we had moved into Kinghorn, and by the day after my arrival I'd begun to forge friendships which I hoped would last a lifetime. Straight away The Wee Shoppe became a regular focal point for our life in Fife and certainly colours our fond memories of our time there.

CHAPTER 7

Pettycur ~ Kinghorn to Kirkcaldy

Letting Go

Ode to Pettycur Bay
You charmed us with your beauty -
Mesmerising silver-splashed sea
and endless rippling sands.
Ancient harbour of days gone by
Where travellers harken the Criers cry.
Tiny fishing boats, sheds and mosaics to delight,
A blend of old and new hides memories
of industry, people and age old stories,
whose moments in time
changed the course of Scotland's plight.
Yet the sands, sea, sun and winds remain forever
Pettycur.

OUR FIRST DAY at Pettycur, the following Monday, was a bit dreamy, much like you feel when you arrive on holiday, relieved to reach your destination but you just want to drop everything and explore. We were fortunate to live on the third and top floor of a small apartment block over-looking Pettycur Beach. My eyes followed the coastline along the craggy cliff-face, topped with traditional green caravans, towards Burntisland. This day was particularly clear so we could even see The Forth Rail Bridge in the distance. The hills and vales on the far banks of the Forth completed the panoramic scene.

This view across the Forth ebbed and flowed with both time and tide in an ever changing landscape, from the crisp yellow glow of early morning to the burnt orange hues of sunset. We could not see Edinburgh from our window but when we took a stroll down to Pettycur Harbour the city was just opposite, as if completing the picture – a water-colour artist's delight! This was certainly a magical place and I felt truly blessed.

After that first day my husband went back to work and I filled my early days with cleaning, making our flat a home and getting to know the local facilities. A week overflowing with activity meant I barely had time to think. I acquired a habit early on, of taking at least one walk per day, an essential part of my orientation process to become familiar with my new surroundings. Behind us were the cliff steps - a challenge to walk in one go. Then there was the sharper climb from the beach to The Bay Hotel, or alternatively the gentle stroll up Pettycur Road which swept towards the village. From there, little back streets and winding paths took me various ways down to Kinghorn Harbour and the lifeboat station, one of the hubs of village life. My level of fitness was enhanced greatly, as was my sense of well being.

A week sped by before the need to continue my personal journey compelled me to walk the coastal path between Kinghorn and Kirkcaldy, our nearest large town. Just above Kinghorn harbour, following the coastal path signs, I took a tunnel under a railway which led behind Kinghorn caravans.

Before long I was walking on a more natural coastal path following the rocky shore. Occasional ruins appeared just above the water's edge, reminders of local ship builders. Hand-cleaved rock pools were clearly visible too - wash pools for the railway construction workers and almost certainly enjoyed by local children in more recent times. Well maintained steps, slopes and a zig-zag path passed small pebbled inlets which led to Seafield Tower, an imposing 16th Century ruin - one of many scattered along this coast adding interest and intrigue. Looking down towards the tower I paused for a few moments enjoying the view over the water to North Berwick. Suddenly movement on the rocks near-by caught my attention. Did that rock flap and slither? Were those splashes more than just waves hitting the shingle?

I was jubilant. This was my first memorable sighting of seals - so close to civilisation, too. I raised my camera but the animals kept diving out of sight or lying so still that they were barely indistinguishable from their bed of rock.

I strolled towards the tower and sat on a large boulder, as close to the seals as I dare, mesmerised by their antics, until suddenly I felt a damp fishy breath, as if someone had dared to creep up on me in my reverie and brush past, his face barely inches from my own. I glanced around to find a 'man' settling on a rock nearby, his alluring face and deep brown eyes gazing into my own. I might have been smitten by his sensuous touch or unnerved by his audacity to invade my space, if it hadn't been for an over-riding fishy scent which made me smile.

'Hi,' I said, as casually as anyone could, face to face with a Selkie, whilst stifling a giggle. No, not a Selfie, I'm not that vain. A Selkie! The seal-man turned away as if disappointed by my nonchalance and peered over his shoulder as he slipped back towards the sea, his round eyes full of heartbreak and rejection.

'Please wait,' I said, 'I'm sorry, but you startled me.' His eyes flickered behind long lashes.

'Well, I might,' he said, lounging on the nearest rock and gazing at me intently. I shuffled, avoiding his unnerving glare. He seemed to relax at my embarrassment. I took courage and stared back. Before me was a handsome man, early 50's with extremely short soft brown hair with wisps of white and, unusually so, he wore a long feathery moustache. I stifled another laugh as it dawned on me that he was certainly quite seal-like.

Undeterred he moved closer, reaching out for my hands. He grasped them between his cold damp fingers and pulled me close. I was adrift in the moment, overwhelmed by a sense of lost, unrequited and rejected love, as if my past, present and future feelings and desires all rolled into one, washed away on the waves.

He let go and blinked at me, holding the silent moment in his deep brown gaze.

'Let go,' he said, pausing for effect, 'is my message for you.' Then he was gone. My eyes watered. Suddenly desolate, I was aware only of my loneliness. As my salty tears fell into a rock pool below, each droplet shed a great burden.

A few moments later a lone seal slipped into the sea. I sighed; a hint of relief seeping into my soul.

It was with lighter but thoughtful steps that I continued towards my destination. Shopping seemed incongruous to the moment, so I headed directly to the station to catch the train home. Home? It is strange how excited I was to be returning to Pettycur, my adopted home.

Ode to my Selkie
Rakish, handsome
We met quite by chance,
With your sea faring nonchalance
Yet boyish sensitivity
You charmed me
by your words of simplicity.
The depths of your round brown eyes
Pierced the history
Of my heart's deepest mystery.
Shedding your human form
You slid back into the sea.
As I shed a huge burden
Setting me free.

It was several days until I ventured forth again, no pun intended. There was actually no real need to go far, because everything was within a mile or so. Within ten minutes walk I could reach a butchers, bakers, The Co-op, Savers Supermarket, a Deli, a bank machine, not to mention a doctors, dentist, library and community centre and various cafes. Yes, even my car felt neglected, and yet if it needed attention there were no less than two car garages in Kinghorn. An amazing place.

CHAPTER 8

Pettycur

Thankful for the Here and Now

AS DAYLIGHT HOURS were diminishing I became restless. I'd been reading an account of the history of Kinghorn the night before; intriguing but not necessarily conducive to a good night's sleep. In my first few weeks here I had slept soundly, waking fully refreshed every morning, but after a short visit to Bedfordshire I began suffering from tension headaches and sleepless nights again. I sighed, thinking wistfully that I had left those days down south a couple of months before.

My days here followed a pattern. After my husband left for work at 6.30am I usually spent an hour or so surfing the internet and checking emails before getting dressed. Then my morning's writing activities were sacrosanct, after which invariably I would go for a walk or meet one of my new friends for a chat.

This day was different. Within minutes I was up and ready to leave, walking briskly up the steps towards the graveyard. The moonlight's reflection glimmered on the Forth below, the lights of Burntisland still bright in the distance. Turning away into the misty gloom I shivered, feeling the spirits of many a witch who had met their death at that very spot. Undeterred

I continued towards Burntisland Road. I had an appointment to keep. Once I reached my intended destination, a monument to King Alexander III, I gazed upon the place where this King of Scotland met his death; his story echoed in my consciousness. I had learnt that this young King had died, not in combat but through losing his way on a foggy night and tumbling over the cliff. Determined not to suffer the same fate I moved away from the edge, paused and took a photo towards the lights of Edinburgh. Glancing over my shoulder I noticed a figure cloaked in green moving towards me. I froze as this young, pretty maiden passed me by.

'Have you seen my husband?' her voice whimpered, but she did not wait for my reply but continued as if floating down the path. The hint of sunrise caught my eye across the bay behind Pettycur Harbour and when I turned back the lady had vanished into the morning mist. Guessing her to be Yolande, the late king's young wife, I decided to follow her, making my way past The Bay Hotel and down towards Burntisland. Spotting a path under the railway beside The Sands Hotel, I found myself walking on the shore once more. The sky was spectacular. I didn't see the lady again but her words echoed in my mind.

Although I was lonely at times, unlike this stranger whose loss was great and inexplicable, I was so fortunate to have a husband who worked hard each day so that we could enjoy this unique life. We spent every weekend as if it was a holiday and in the evenings we often took a stroll along the bay and around the harbour before supper. It was idyllic and I was truly thankful.

'Oh no,' I cried, suddenly realising that water was seeping through my trainers. Without thinking I had taken the direct route across the sands back towards 'home' which I could clearly see in the distance. The saying goes that if the tide is out beyond Black Rock at the start of your walk, you should be able to reach Pettycur before the tide catches you out. What the guide book does not say is that it's best to wear waterproof boots regardless!

Thankfully I reached Pettycur Beach in safety and since the sun had now pierced through the mist I sat on a rock and took my shoes off to dry, my toes resting in the soft sand. Black Rock was now surrounded by water in the distance to my right. I sat in the sunshine watching the tide come in, channels of water seeping across the sand flats at quite a pace. I reached into my pocket for my trusty camera and took a snap before letting my head rest back on the rocks. I must have nodded off briefly, but was soon awakened by a cry from the cliff tops above to my left. I looked up, hoping to see my lady in green, but instead a man in strange garb was standing on where I later came to know as Crying Hill, where travellers were warned of the imminent arrival of an incoming ferry from Leith, Edinburgh. The man was pointing out to sea and a large old-fashioned ferry boat was heading towards the tiny harbour, its tall black funnel pumping out steam-like cloudlets into an otherwise clear blue sky. On the track above the harbour passengers were alighting from a carriage and a man was unloading barrels from a horse and trap.

Water now surrounded the rock on which I sat and so I had to pick up my trainers and paddle through the shallows to the shore. I headed toward the harbour where I put on my footwear and stood on the cobbles watching the ferry men tying it securely and the passengers alight. After several minutes it was time for those waiting near me to walk up the tiny gangway. It was 11.45 am.

'One and six if you're travelling to Leith, madam?' a man asked, holding his hand out to help me aboard.

'No thank you. I'm not ready to travel back south just yet,' I replied.

'After today you'll have to go to Burntisland, madam. Today is your last chance from Pettycur.'

'Not to worry sir,' I replied. 'It must be 1842,' I added aloud - to which the sailor frowned. Losing interest he was soon busy aiding the barrel man, my presence forgotten. I walked back along the harbour and down on to the now narrow stretch of shingle.

'Healing waters lady?' a young lad asked, holding a cup out to me.

Suddenly extremely thirsty, I drank greedily, at first not noticing his hand held out. I placed a pound coin in his palm, but ignored his plea after me,

'Hey lady, what's this? You can be hanged for counterfeit coinage!' but when I turned he had gone, as too had the ferry, replaced by a blue and white fishing boat and a couple of colourful rowing boats. I smiled, feeling totally refreshed. Glancing up I noticed that there was a small stream of water trickling down the rocks and birds stood at its mouth drinking. It's a sign that the spring must be fresh, I thought.

Back in the flat I filled the kettle. Time for a nice cup of tea and to sit and enjoy the view. After a few minutes I turned on my PC and wrote:

1286 King Meets his Maker

King Alexander III married Yolande de Dreux in 1285 in the hopes of gaining a rightful heir. Only a year later he was returning to her side in Kinghorn in the Kingdom of Fife, when tragedy struck. He lost his way on a dark night and, falling from his horse, he plunged down the cliff to the beach at Pettycur.

Alexander's dying wish for an heir to his throne was thwarted even after death when Yolande gave birth but her child was still-born. This loss prompted battles and wars culminating with the deadly Wars of Independence with England.

I reflected that we were fortunate that the ballot box of today's independence vote (2014) was far more civilised. Mind you, it was strange that such an insignificant act as putting a cross on a piece of paper could define the future of nations. A few months from then Scotland would have the chance to be free from England for the first time in 300 years. I was living up north during interesting times and felt privileged to be living in Fife as the debate heated up.

As to myself, I was grateful to Yolande who had helped me to gain a better perspective on my life, and also to the sailor who made me realise that I had no wish to return south - not yet anyway.

Before switching off my PC I typed:

1842 Last Pettycur to Leith Ferry
Although the sluice gates at Pettycur proved to be effective in ensuring Pettycur Pier was navigable, the deep water pier completed in Burntisland in 1838 was deemed to be a more viable route from Edinburgh to Fife. Thus the Stage Coach has been rerouted and the last ferry steamed away from Pettycur Harbour at midday today.

CHAPTER 9

East Wemyss to Buckhaven

A New Vision ~ Challenged

THE DICHOTOMY BETWEEN my life here in Fife and my life down in Bedfordshire was significant. I travelled down south once a month, the days full of frenzied activity - seeing my parents and family, catching up with close friends, taking part in book promotions, checking on the house and doing innumerable jobs to keep everything safe. Up in Fife my time was spent predominantly alone writing, although I made a few friends and volunteered for a couple of groups, which I will describe in more detail later. Although I enjoyed being immersed in my old life in a small village near Bedford, I admit that I felt childishly excited on my return to Pettycur, impatient for the journey to be over. I only wish I could overcome the anomaly of sometimes finding it difficult to settle once I'd arrived. Why?

In October I had just finished proof reading the manuscript of my murder mystery. Also, I had come to the end of pre-arranged face to face promotions for my historical fiction. I had not, however, planned what I was going to do next with my time. Writing the third in my trilogy seemed strange since the settings were The Channel Islands,

Southampton and Brooklands – far removed from my present reality.

As the days were becoming shorter and Christmas approached my husband's hours at work also increased. This gave rise to long periods of time enjoying my own company. I dabbled with a book cover, kept paperwork up to date and shuffled my various projects around aimlessly.

'You're having a wee wobble,' one of my new dear friends said.

'You'll be fine,' said another. 'It's understandable you're unsettled, going back and forth like that.'

That weekend I was struck by the idea for this novella. It was a glorious day in November and Richard and I were walking between East Wemyss and Buckhaven. It was so mild that we even took off our outer coats. As we walked past the last cottages, we paused to read the boards telling us the history of the East Wemyss Caves which we were soon to pass - caverns set deep in the red rock. We did not pause long to admire them but continued up steep steps which passed the remains of the castle of Macduff, of William Shakespeare fame. The path climbed beside the remains of its ancient walls. Momentarily I rested my hand on an exposed surface. I shivered with the realisation of connected history.

Once at the top we followed what used to be a railway track to Buckhaven. The path was easy and the views over the Forth full of dappled reflected sunlight on the waters, which we glimpsed between trees and shrubs. Unfortunately we could find no welcome cafe as we entered Buckhaven. Maybe our search would have been more fruitful if we had ventured further. Instead we retraced our steps, deciding that the caves warranted another visit one day, but on a guided tour maybe. The walk and fresh air had certainly lifted our spirits.

On our return to East Wemyss I turned and took a photo of the wind turbine you could see in the distance. It was strange because when I looked at the view finder the whole structure had vanished. Puzzled, I took another shot. It was as if the structure had not been built at all. I showed my husband, who tried to imagine a scientific explanation for my mystery.

'Perhaps it's light reflecting paint,' Richard suggested, but I was both confused and excited by this phenomenon, that my camera had taken me back to a time before the contraption was built. At that moment the idea for this novella was born. It happened just like that.

I had already been penning a diary which included muddled historical facts I'd gleaned as I searched for information about the area where we were now living, but now my thoughts began to develop form and purpose. While I waited patiently for feedback on my murder mystery from my beta readers I would continue my journal, but also begin some serious research. Back at the flat I devoured all the guide books we possessed and then took my first trip to the local history section of Kirkcaldy library, where an afternoon passed in a moment. I studied people, saints and even ghosts and fairy tales famous in Fife. Questions formed.

Who would I love to meet if only I could? Which places had historical significance? The answer to that was rather –

which didn't? The wonderful thing about fiction is that anything is possible.

The project began to take shape but in early December I headed back down south again, a shorter visit this time of only three days, but all the more intense. The journey back north was fractious - delayed planes, missed buses and trains running late, all adding to my frustrations. By the time I had trundled my case down the road to Pettycur, it was dark and raining quite heavily. It was only 4pm. The following day, Friday, my face was red and I thought I'd caught a chill, my tension headaches had returned. Sadly I had to miss the Friday Lunch Club Christmas party where I volunteered at a lunch for the over 60's - a place where I gained far more from chatting to both members and volunteers than they ever did from the odd plate I cleared away or cup of tea I served. Volunteering was often like that.

The following day I felt much better and my sense of well-being had returned. I had enjoyed tea with one of my new friends where we chatted for England, or Scotland maybe. That Saturday evening Richard and I enjoyed a delicious supper at The Ship in Kinghorn with our new neighbours. Then on the Sunday old friends from Linlithgow visited for coffee at The Carousel, a cafe overlooking Kinghorn Harbour. After we had waved them goodbye we headed down to the harbour and yes, we sat drinking a cup of tea in mid December al fresco. Mad I know, but the sun was breaking through and the company was great.

Alex and Moira run the Wee Shoppe, which is often open come rain or shine, and they are always cheerful and welcoming. Soon Alex and I realised that we had a common interest - historical fiction - and he loaned me several novels by Nigel Tranter, all set in Scotland of course. This author was a true historian and story teller, a gift which shines through his novels, not in fashion so much in today's literature but one I feel sure will return. After all, story-telling is part of our heritage, without which we would know little of our history.

It was while we were sitting at the harbour one day, when my husband was deep in conversation with a local about the pro's and con's of Scottish Independence, that I took a photo of The Wee Shoppe. I turned, just as Nigel Tranter came to take the seat next to me. He cleared his throat gaining my full attention.

'I hear you like my books,' he said with a smile.

'Oh yes,' I replied, no longer shocked by my visions, 'It's been a pleasure to read them and a great way to learn so much about the fascinating history of Scotland too.'

'I also hear that you are writing a novel set in Fife.'

I blushed. 'Well, it's only a novella; I'm writing for enjoyment really. I think local people might like it but the book could also encourage more visitors to this lovely part of Great Britain.'

'Ah well,' he said, stroking his chin, 'As long as you're not purporting to be writing Historical Fiction in the area.'

'What do you mean?' My face tightened against the perceived criticism. 'I love the area.'

'It's like this. When I wrote about Scotland, and Fife especially, I was writing not just from the heart but from the soul.'

I waited for further explanation but none was offered. 'Can you explain?' I asked.

'When you read my books you are interested in the people and familiar landmarks and begin to form a picture of what it might have been like from your current experience. Isn't that right?'

'Yes it is, but what's wrong with that?'

'The difference between you and me is,' he paused, 'when I write about characters and places I am in a position of knowledge and familiarity. After all, I've lived in Scotland most of my life and over the years I've read numerous detailed historical accounts - some conflicting. I've trodden these paths a hundred times and sought out old photos and paintings depicting how it was or might have been.'

'I understand that, but I'm writing from the point of view of a visitor. I certainly do not claim to be an expert. Anyway, if you live in an area like this you are sometimes blind to its beauty and can take its rich history for granted.'

'I agree Diana, and I have also gleaned enough about you to know that research for your last novel 'Ancasta' was substantial and checked thoroughly by experts.' I blushed again, thrilled that he knew so much about me. He continued, his stern face unwavering. 'I just wanted to give you a gentle warning, but some encouragement too. This journey cannot be all smiles and back patting. Otherwise your head would swell too large for that woolly hat of yours,' and then he vanished, my face almost the shade of my head gear - fuchsia pink!

After he'd gone I was full of more questions. I so wished he'd stayed to talk a little more. Unfortunately, instead of learning from his wisdom, my confidence dipped for a while as the darkness increased in my surroundings. I was flooded with a sense of loss, writing with little heart, let alone soul. On occasions I even longed to be back 'home' in Bedfordshire, and to turn my back on this wonderful opportunity. What right did I have to be writing about Fife?

9ᵗʰ January 2000 The Death of a Truly Scottish Author

Author and historian Nigel Tranter died today. He was a prolific writer of Scottish Historical Fiction reflecting his lifelong interest in the colourful past of Scottish Castles. With his deep understanding of Scottish history and its impact on the present day he was also a renowned speaker in his field, both in the UK and in the USA. Tranter leaves us with a fine legacy of his numerous best-selling novels, including 'Union of the Crowns.'

Wouldn't it be wonderful if I left such a legacy behind me too?

CHAPTER 10

Pettycur

The Sun

Ode to the Sun

Your rays welcome the new day
Yellowy orange seeping into the grey horizon.
A water-colour blot on canvas, ever increasing
until
Your winter sunshine dispels the gloom
Your reflection echoing your warmth,
Reaching across the sea
Life giving, spirit lifting and free.

IT WAS EXACTLY a week after meeting Mr Tranter, only a few days before Christmas that I came to my senses. So many posts on Facebook and Twitter were about 'winter blues,' dark days and stormy nights that I decided to banish my gloomy thoughts by a stomp along the beach.

It wasn't a very promising morning. Dark grey rain or maybe snow filled clouds were drifting at speed overhead from the west and not one soul had ventured out, as far as I could see. I donned on my dark cerise pink gloves and woolly hat, thick socks and wellington boots and headed towards the harbour with the excuse that I had a bag of recycling stuff to put in the large bin there.

Oh wonderful sun!!! From the vantage point of the harbour car-park I glimpsed the sunrise. It was in moments like those that I realised why the ancients and many moderns today worship the sun. Through the cool wind I could feel her warmth from across the Forth above Edinburgh, highlighting the island of Inchkeith and sending reflective rays of cheerfulness rippling over the waves towards me. I stood perfectly still for several minutes, lifting my face to her and smiled. It was **so** good.

Revitalised, I turned and strolled down to the beach. Now in shadow I was quickly engulfed by the piercing wind-chill factor. Was Burntisland rain-swept ahead of me? She was certainly beneath the gloom. Undeterred, I strode out to the water's edge and, leaving the harbour's protection, I was rewarded ten-fold as the sun streamed towards me once more. Mesmerised, I paddled for a while with my back to the wind. Alone, yet content.

I didn't meet a stranger from past times today and yet fortune fell my way to be greeted by the Sun, who from the beginning of time on earth has been life-giving, full of light. The message she passed on to me was,

'If you take a few steps beyond your comfort zone you will be rewarded intensely.'

Historians tell us that in a tiny place called Dunino, three miles from St Andrews, Fife, a stone circle once stood to worship the Celtic Sun God Bel. In the graveyard close by, there is a ninth century rectangular stone, on which is carved a sundial. This

is believed to be either an early Christian symbol or a Druid's altar.

CHAPTER 11

Rosslyn Chapel

Be Wary of Jealousy and Pride

CHRISTMAS WAS A whirl of events in Pettycur. We were blessed, much to our surprise, that family travelled from Bedfordshire and France to be in Edinburgh, only an hour away. On the Sunday before Christmas they came by train to Kinghorn - a rail journey I can recommend which takes you across the famous Forth Rail Bridge and along the charming coastline. We experienced every season that day but I was so glad that the sun shone over Kinghorn Harbour for a wee while too. I cooked Cullen Skink and 'Collups of Beef,' recipes gleaned from a little Scottish cook-book.

'What might they be?' asked our local butcher, obviously amused. After some explanation he cut some rounds of beef for us and I must say that they were deliciously tender after several hours in our newly acquired slow cooker. Richard called it my best purchase in Scotland because it cooked wonderful stews and soups to perfection, with very little effort. When he arrived home late a wholesome broth made an ideal supper, accompanied by a fresh crusty butter filled roll from the bakers.

On Christmas Day, after a wee walk to see Kinghorn Harbour, we drove over to Edinburgh with the help of the Sat

Nav. (what on earth did we do without them and Google maps?) We enjoyed a light-hearted day of good food and excellent wine (except for me because I was driving.) Our menu was an unusual mix of traditions with paté de foie gras and Sauternes from France, followed by roast pork - a favourite of my niece's husband from Uganda and to complete the meal we enjoyed mince pies and cream. Well, we had to have something British didn't we? Not a Brussels sprout or turkey in sight.

On Boxing Day we met up with the family at Rosslyn Chapel, of Da Vinci Code fame. We mused over intricately carved pillars and gargoyles, which we were itching to photograph, but it was not permitted. Apparently someone had fallen down a shallow step whilst taking his shot and then sued the chapel - a sad sign of our age of 'blame culture.'

Two of the pillars near the altar caught my full attention. The information read that an apprentice was waiting for his master to return from an inspiration-seeking trip to Europe when he had a dream. Fired up by the dragons of his imagination, he set to work and completed a masterpiece. His master was extremely jealous when he returned, incensed that his protégé was skilled enough to produce such a remarkable design. In a rage he killed his apprentice but then he was hanged for the deed!

I was just gazing at this pillar, longing to caress the indentations but fingering my camera instead, when I felt a tap on my shoulder. A young man smiled at me. He was wearing a beige tunic, tied around the waist by a brown cord.

'Be guarded of the jealousy of some, but keep faith. Listen to those who believe in you without losing your head to pride!'

Then he vanished from whence he had come. That night I wrote in my journal:

The Da Vinci Code Factor ~ April 2008

Rosslyn Chapel announced an unprecedented increase in visitors since the film 'The Da Vinci Code' was released last year. They peaked at over one hundred and fifty thousand! The public's curiosity about the link between Freemasonry and the chapel's three pillars continues to cause controversy. Historians despair at the line crossed from history to fantasy, egged on by the power of commercialism, muddying the waters of truth.

Oh dear, I thought, where did that leave my Fife Fantasy? How many historians will I upset along the way with this novel? I wondered.

CHAPTER 12

Burntisland and Pettycur

A Guid Scottish New Year

'THAT WAS LOVELY beef we had on Saturday,' I remarked as our local butcher cut some lamb chops for us, the day after Boxing Day.

'That's good. Are you doing anything nice on New Year's Eve?' he asked, his smile full of Scottish mirth.

'We wanted to have a truly Scottish Hogmanay since it was our first, but we also have a friend to stay with us who certainly needs lots of good cheer for 2014, so my husband has kindly booked for us to go to The Kingswood Hotel on Burntisland Road for a meal and a Ceilidh. I expect you are planning a special evening too.'

'Oh yes, but it's nothing like when I was younger. In those days it was great fun.' He paused as another customer entered the shop.

'I'd love you to tell me one day,' I replied as I headed for the door.

On New Year's Eve I was a bit nervous, to tell you the truth. After all, Scottish people know how to dance, don't they? I was prepared to be entertained rather than to participate, but the 'caller' had other ideas. We were delighted to watch kilted dancers expertly twirling their ladies with aplomb, but felt relief to see a few folks, whose memory had slipped since last year, who were nearly as uncoordinated as we were. Great fun was had by all. The meal was lovely too, and at midnight we all piled out on to the patio to be treated to a free firework display, courtesy of Edinburgh just across the water.

At about half past midnight, having travelled up by train from the south of England that day, our friend was tired and so we left early. I imagine that the evening ended with Auld Lang Syne.

Once we were back at Pettycur I suggested that the others went on in.

'I'll be up in a minute,' I said, strolling to the path above the bay. Standing still in my glad rags, one of my favourite dresses of salmon and earthy colours with a hint of sequins, I hummed the tune, thinking of new friends and old ones as I took a photo of the lights of Burntisland across the bay - the vast stretch of sands basking in the crisp moonlight, pools of light reflecting its glory.

Within moments a familiar figure ran down the path from nowhere, or at least he seemed familiar and his voice reminded me of our friendly local butcher - always cheerful and happy to share a tale or two.

'You have so many questions Diana and you asked about Hogmanay. Come with me and I'll show you.'

'But I only have my thin evening dress on.'

In that instant I looked down and instead I was wearing jeans and a thick duffle coat, one like I remember wearing in my late teens.

'Don't ask questions, just come with me. I'm Andrew,' he said as he took me by the hand. 'Have you got any coins in your pockets?'

I took off my mittens and felt in both pockets, pulling out three five pence pieces - not the silly little ones we have today but the old kind, about the size of our current 10p.

'I've got these,' I replied.

'They'll do. Now, when the door opens, offer one to your host as a gift before you set foot in the house, but don't forget to let me go in first.'

Andrew pulled me towards a door where the window was blazing with light which spilled out into the front garden. I heard the church bells strike twelve.

'A Guid New Year!' Andrew exclaimed as the door was opened wide and a gent in a green, black and red kilt and his wife came to greet us, both young with a symbol of newly-weds over their door. Andrew handed over a piece of coal before stepping over the threshold and in the light I noticed for the first time how handsome he was. After our host slapped him on the back in a gesture of friendship, Andrew produced a bottle of malt from his pocket and we were both ushered inside - the wife grinning as I placed a coin in the palm of her hand before stepping on to her mat. She hugged me as if I was kin before placing it on the mantle-piece, an aroma of cinnamon and fruit wafting around the spotless room.

Others soon arrived, some with shortbread and children with cake. All enjoyed the vittels and a wee dram and then our host struck up a chorus of 'Auld Lang Syne' before we made our way back out into the night. There was no time for conversation because Andrew caught my hand once more and drew me towards the house opposite. Did I hear the church bells sound out twelve once more? How strange, but I had little time to dwell on this anomaly as a similar ritual was repeated. This time a newly lit log fire was burning apple-wood and pine - fresh, warm and welcoming. This couple were probably in their sixties but in hearty health and as we sang I counted perhaps four generations of their family gathered for the occasion. When a small lad of about five dropped a few crumbs of his cake on the floor his mother rushed to sweep them up and a few minutes later a tableaux of smiling faces bade us farewell.

The third and final time I heard the church chime that night was outside a tiny cottage near the harbour, and before us was a wizened gentleman whose bearded rugged complexion wore signs of many a year at sea - a pipe balanced at the corner of his smiling mouth. The greeting was no less warm, the home just as clean as the last, albeit a touch spartan, but the twinkle in this mariner's eyes as he gave me a kiss of welcome spoke of hidden secrets and memories. We kept the old man company, sitting around his fire, as he shared a tale of when he was a sea captain at Hogmanay.

'I had a heathen crew d'ye ken?' Seeing my puzzled face he added, 'most of them weren't Scottish.' He paused to sip a wee dram and so I echoed him, the brown liquid burning in my throat and making me cough.

He winked at me but after a pause continued. 'I ordered me men to scrub the decks, clean the galley and even their bunk rooms until the wood glowed and the brass shone. They didna half moan but when they'd finished I'd never seen the ship sa clean.' The old sailor smiled taking a slow draught from his pipe.

'Next I gave an order for all of me men to meet on deck just before midnight but at a quarter to twelve me words were forgotten when we saw a flare go up - a plea for help d'ya ken.

All men were on deck to guide our ship towards the flare, ever cautious to remain in safe channels just off the coast of Stonehaven. Anyway, as we approached, the vessel appeared to be perfectly fine, but nevertheless we dropped anchor for the wee vessel to come alongside. To my surprise it was me young nephew and his friend and as they came aboard the crew were delighted to see fireballs lighting up the streets of the wee toon.

Guid New Year Uncle, me nephew exclaimed and we hugged as he placed a lump of coal in me hand as he jumped on deck. We spent a night of merriment, drinking whisky and singing, the likes of which I'd never experienced in any other part of the world and me crew were a bit in awe of the dark haired young visitor who brought us good fortune in their year ahead.'

I was about to ask a question but Old Jack placed his finger on his lips and continued, 'The irony of my tale is that me ship was lost in terrible storm off the coast of Newfoundland only a month later, but the joy of it was that all me men were saved!'

I was sad to leave Old Jack that night but, ever the young gentleman, Andrew saw me back safely to Pettycur, tipsy with kindness and goodwill. I put the key in the door and turned to say thank you but he had disappeared and I was yet again in my finery. As I opened the door my husband was just slipping into bed.

'Enjoy the fresh air?' he asked. 'I would have come too but I had a long day at work yesterday.'

'It was lovely. I really feel as if I've welcomed 2014 in style,' or was it more like 1974 I calculated silently, as I mused on the evening's events – or even maybe 1894 with Old Jack, I puzzled as I slipped into a deep but contented sleep.

Guid New Year

A warm welcome awaits you
Full of Scottish cheer
Centuries of revellers
Exclaim 'A Guid New year.'
Memories befriend you
Traditions held so dear
Generations meet together
To exclaim 'A Guid New Year.'
Hopes for the future
Resolutions made with malt and beer
To drink, to dance to eat to sing
To say, 'A Guid New Year.'

CHAPTER 13

Dysart and Ravenscraig Castle

'The Present is a Gift'

ON THE FIRST Sunday in January it was a bit bleak so we had our breakfast in the Carousel, a cafe overlooking Kinghorn Bay - great food and cheerful staff - ideal if it's just too wet to sit down by the harbour. We also needed space on our own to talk. It was a day of reckoning - time for us to make some decisions about the future. When would Richard retire? How long should we stay in Scotland? Could we bear to leave Kinghorn now that we'd found it? How did we feel about returning to our life down south?

It was as if I held our future balanced in the palm of my hands - on the one hand I held our lives down in Bedfordshire, close to my parents, family and friends in a home we have lovingly restored over the past eight years. On my other hand rested our dream life in Kinghorn, our fledgling love for our new surroundings and especially for its people.

A friend is always saying, *'The present is a gift,'* and that we should leave the future to look after itself. We did try to live on this premise most of the time, but occasionally doubts and fears flooded in. We decided to have this breakfast meeting with the sole intention of making plans, so that we

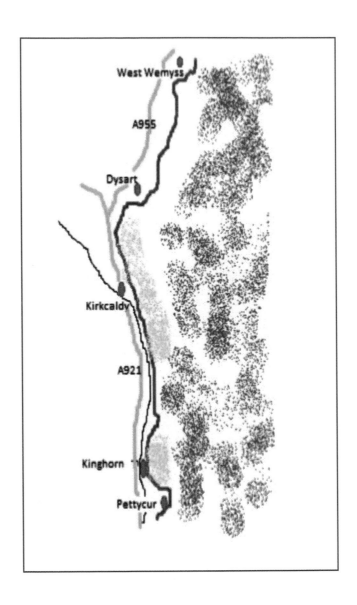

could relax and enjoy our remaining quality time in Scotland – or longer if that was our decision.

'Warrior not Worrier' said my January calendar. The previous night I'd had quite a disturbed sleep though most of the time in Fife we slept extremely well - the air was so crisp and clear, filling our lungs with freshness. Only the occasional whine of a westerly wind disturbed us, as it blew up the Forth from the direction of the rail bridge and whipped around our windows, sometimes seeping into our bedroom.

Personally, I knew I shouldn't fret, but after years of fretting it's a hard habit to break.

We had so many dilemmas.

My husband wished to live by the sea where he was bursting with energy and vitality, whereas, though I loved it in Fife, I struggled with the thought of living so far away from my elderly parents.

Also, could we afford for me to continue to focus on my writing when my husband retired or should I find more reliable paid employment? Was it time to put my dream into action of setting up a publishing cooperative? So many questions.

During the morning we came up with a tentative plan, enabling us to get on with life, but it was a full year before many of the issues we had raised were finally resolved.

After our lengthy discussion we needed some fresh air and exercise so we headed to Dysart. There was an easy walk, that I had noticed on our map, which went back along the coastal path towards Kirkcaldy and then through the park above the beach returning to Dysart. Since it was already nearly 2pm and darkness fell around 3.30, this seemed like the perfect option.

The walk was steeped in natural and historical interest - full of charm too. It led us around the harbour which was once an important port for salt. I was interested to read later that 'Pan Ha,' a restored cottage nearby, refers to the salt pans back in the 13th Century. It is hard to imagine tall sailing ships entering this wee harbour, but they did.

A small tunnel takes you beside the walls of Ravenscraig Castle and the park, making an easy but pleasant amble through wooded areas, with pathways down to secluded beaches in the brow of the walls. We paused to peer through gun slits in the fortifications, towards Kinghorn on the other side of the bay. As you turn the corner to look back towards Kirkcaldy, the sudden view of the castle ruin jolts your consciousness, in stark contrast to the 1960's towers of flats almost beside it.

On reaching Kirkcaldy waterfront we headed back towards the ruins of the castle and through Ravenscraig Park. My husband stopped to take some photos while I strolled on, my eyes drawn to three large trees, which seemed to be speaking to each other in whispers as the leaves rustled overhead.

It was getting dark - in fact there was only a glimmer of light through the canopy. I shivered. It was time to move on because neither of us had brought a torch. When I looked around my husband had disappeared. I was standing at the centre of the triangle formed by the trees when I heard a large cry as if in battle. Quickly I ran to hide, but in the shadows I could just make out a struggle - the clashing of swords and cries of anguish as two dark figures fell. A second later I saw the silhouette of a third man standing over the fallen. He turned just as one of the lifeless forms struggled to sit up one last time and stabbed the remaining warrior in the back. My body was shaking. Never in my life had I witnessed such crimes only a few feet away from where I cowered. I closed my eyes but seconds later jumped with fear as a hand rested on my shoulder.

'It's only me,' my husband said. 'What are you afraid of?'

I looked up and glanced back to see the shape of fallen branches ahead of me where the bodies had been.

'You have such a vivid imagination,' my husband chuckled as he took me by the hand and led me back down the steps towards the harbour.

'What happened back there?' he asked as we sat drinking tea and sharing a scone and jam in the Harbourmaster's House at Dysart harbour.

I paused and wondered what I should tell this man, the geographer and scientist with whom I shared a home. Facts, facts and more facts were all he believed in.

'It's hard to explain, and I'm not sure I even want to try,' I replied.

After our refreshments we had half an hour before they closed to enjoy the excellent exhibition in the basement. It described the historical, environmental and geographical aspects of the Fife Coast - the Coastal Path and its flora and fauna - safe topics between us.

A few days later, as I was carrying out some research in Kirkcaldy library I came across this legend:

Murder or Unfortunate Mistaken Identity
In the late nineteenth century there were three brothers of the Stirling family living in Ravenscraig Castle. One night they came across each other in the darkness near their home. Thinking each other was a burglar they fought and all were killed. Afterwards three trees were planted just where they had fallen.

I shivered yet again as I read this account. What shadows did we wrestle with on dark nights? Even in daylight hours did we perceive things differently? Could words be misinterpreted or hide the truth?

The following weekend, our wedding anniversary, we travelled to Braemar and from the road across the Cairngorms I saw people skiing for the first time in real life. The view from the hotel was magical.

On the first morning back at Pettycur I looked out of the window and thought there was snow on the beach. It was actually a trick of the light. I know because I put my wellies on to go and check.

The less kind weather in the days that followed prompted us to be tourists and take the train to Edinburgh, only forty minutes away from Kinghorn Station. We visited The National Gallery, The Royal Mile and Edinburgh Castle and we walked up to the City Observatory at Calton Hill to look back over the

Forth towards Burntisland and Kinghorn, each of us pointing in the direction we thought was 'home.'

One personal frustration was an embargo on making personal comments about our life in Fife on Twitter, Facebook and on my blog. Just think of the posts and tweets I might have shared had I been able to:

'We stood on Calton Hill today and looked across the Forth to Kinghorn,' had to be 'We stretched our legs and enjoyed lovely scenery.'

'Hey, look at this beautiful sunset over Burtisland,' became 'lovely sunset this evening.'

'We walked along the coastal path today between Dysart and West Wemyss,' was rather 'great to have a brisk walk today.'

'There's this lovely warm and welcoming cafe called The Walk Inn with fresh sea food,' was the more bland, 'had fresh fish for lunch today.'

(The Walk Inn is now a welcoming pub but the cafe is called The Suburban Pantry and can be found near the museum behind the Inn – November 2016)

'We are at The Silver Sands Cafe where you have a good view of the bay and the Forth towards Edinburgh. Nice food too,' had to be the alternative version, 'Enjoyed lunch out today. Chilli and baked potatoes.'

'I read about The Eden Estuary today - a wildlife sanctuary in the north east of Fife and I long to go to see the seals there,' was replaced by 'looking forward to feeding time of the seals.'

The posts did not hide the reality, just generalised and stretched the truth. I was bursting to say so much, but I couldn't. You see, our house was empty down south and we couldn't bear to put the property up for rent. We'd spent the last eight years renovating it to make a home we were proud of. Helpful neighbours and relations were keeping a close eye, but to advertise that it was empty to the world was not prudent. (Note to any burglar: By the time you read this we will be back down south or have moved up to Fife permanently.)

I also remembered St Margaret's words of warning and the need for secrecy.

CHAPTER 14

Dysart to West Wemyss

Hard Work Canna Kill Anyone

OUR NEXT WALK along The Fife Coastal Trail was from Dysart to West Wemyss. The cobbled road down to the car park at the Harbourmaster's House is not far out of Kirkcaldy but it is on this stretch of path that you have choices. You either walk both ways or you need to find out about the buses for your return. Up until this point on our adventures, we could catch a train back to the car, but at Kirkcaldy the track veers inland. This in no problem really because, once equipped with an up-to-date bus timetable, it is easy to hop on and off between villages.

There are many routes out of Dysart with walks beside the rocky beach, ambling over the brow of the hill and out on to a playing field at the top, or by walking through the tiny back streets. All lead to the same point - the memorial to Frances Colliery which had seams of coal running underneath the Forth. The only remnants of those industrial days is the iconic red tower and lift shaft wheel which are right next to the coastal path, opposite an area of reclaimed cliff top grassland.

This path continues above the sea line, beside a meadow and then through a tiny spinney at the edge of which is a bench where you may pause a while, especially on a sunny day. Here we were surprised to look out towards West Wemyss, which appeared like a Mediterranean village nestled along the coast, reminiscent of Portmeirion. Overhanging branches framed the view of the village, harbour and ever changing sea. Once refreshed we took the steep slippery steps to the shore below, taking care to place each foot firmly at a time.

From then onwards it was easy. The path takes you along the walls of the Wemyss family graveyard, at the end of which is a blocked off tunnel. I paused for a while to take a photo.

I felt a light tap on my arm and turned to find a lady, short but stocky - her long dress blackened with what I guessed was coal dust. There were no polite introductions.

'Folla me,' she commanded and so I did, noticing that my trainers had disappeared, as had my jeans, replaced by a long brown skirt and blouse, not dissimilar to those of my guide - a beige scarf over my head.

I followed this woman, her head bowed down and back bent, into the entrance to the cave where she handed me a holder and lit the candle before beckoning me further into the gloom. My eyes soon adjusted to the flickering light but I found it hard to keep up, my feet slipping on the wet uneven floor. The noises built up around me - bangs and rumbles echoing in the dark. Instinctively I covered my face with my scarf, the coal dust making me cough as its astringent molecules reached my lungs. I paused a moment to catch my breath – virtually impossible in this airless place - as my guide brushed past me back from whence we'd come, waving for me to follow her,

'Hurry ye up lass,' she called back as I turned, noticing the load of coal she was carrying in a basket on her back. Three times I repeated this trail, my hands now black. Inadvertently I brushed my skirt, the coal dust smudging my clothes, the blackness holding firm.

'Enough,' I called out when out in the open again. I gasped for breath.

My guide woman laughed heartily in my face, her hands gripping both sides of her straightening back before a sudden frown furrowed her brow.

'Ye canna ken what 'ard work is like lass, 'til yuv been down ther, but 'ard work is guid!'

Then her scowl returned into a toothless grin before she headed back into the cave.

'Bye the noo,' echoed in the cave entrance.

I sat down on a large boulder for a while breathing deeply and stared out to sea. Maybe I've never really known what true hard work is, I mused, with all my moaning and groaning in the past - a sober lesson to reflect on.

Realising that Richard was much further along the path, I rushed to catch up with him and as we continued our stroll into the charming village of West Wemyss I tried to think of parallel elements of hardship in my life, but I was thankful that I could think of none so extreme. At the end of the path along the bay we reached the harbour, which once saw trade the likes of which are hard to imagine in this sleepy backwater of painted houses and stepped roofs. In fact West Wemyss, like the coastal part of Dysart, is picture perfect and lovingly restored. We headed for the cafe, The Walk Inn - an exciting community project we'd heard of, where a disused pub has been turned into a bistro cafe with an art gallery, run by local people and volunteers. I was struck by how eerily quiet it was along the street - hardly a car moving and no sign of life behind blinds or curtains. It reminded me of some coastal villages down in the south west of England, where more than every other house was a holiday rental and the life of the place has been sucked out. Mind you it *was* January!

I can imagine when the mines closed that the heart of the community was broken; generations of families and their heritage directionless. Does this suffering still vibrate behind wooden doors and within stone walled cottages? Was the final blow the closing of the village pub, once the hub of community life? I admire those who have built up the business at the Walk Inn, now renowned for excellent food and a warm welcome, and I hope it goes some way to bringing neighbours closer as well as being an excellent 'stop off' for folks like us, visitors enjoying the coastal trail. I also hope that local people will move back into the area and that it will not be totally full of second home owners - Edinburgh folks maybe or people from further away, delighted to have a retreat from the city.

When I paused to read the inscription on a memorial nearby I became fully absorbed in the sombre atmosphere of the place. Did I feel a chill as I stood deep in thought or was it just the winter wind?

Later I wrote:

Tragedy Leads to Mine Closure
The panning of salt and the mining of coal have been key
industries in Fife from as early as the sixteenth century. It was
a sad day when the mine at East Wemyss was closed in 1967,
but it was not due to exhaustion of the natural resource,
viability or even the well documented Miners' Strike but due to
a tragic fire in 1967 which resulted in the death of nine men.
There is a memorial to the men who died, as a stark reminder
of the dangers they faced during every working day.

Time heals they say, and these villages are very pretty. -
rich in history and natural charm, not to mention the good
cheer in the cafés. The sea and tranquillity certainly calms the
spirit too.

CHAPTER 15

West Wemyss to East Wemyss

A Garden – 'A Thing of Beauty and a Job Forever'

LIFE HAD SETTLED down into a routine since Christmas. Emails, orders, Facebook and Twittering from 6.30 to about 8.30 am, often snuggled in bed with a cup of tea unless I had any washing to put on. I'd sometimes compile a blog post during that time too.

Once up it was time to be creative – writing, reading, researching, making notes, merging diary with facts, fantasy with reality. I was beginning to live in the present - to walk on the beach when it was sunny and stop a wee while to watch the sea and the ever changing colours and shapes of the clouds, or to follow the path of ships, large and small as they traversed along the Forth, wondering where they were heading. Occasionally though, my thoughts would return to life in Bedfordshire. Whilst living a dream I'm told that there are always sacrifices to be made and one was my garden. This was why the next part of our walk was so pertinent to my own life both here in Fife and down in Bedfordshire since it helped to resolve a small part of the dilemmas we both faced.

A week later we decided to walk along the coast between West Wemyss and East Wemyss, the next part of the Fife Coastal Trail but this time we followed the route in reverse.

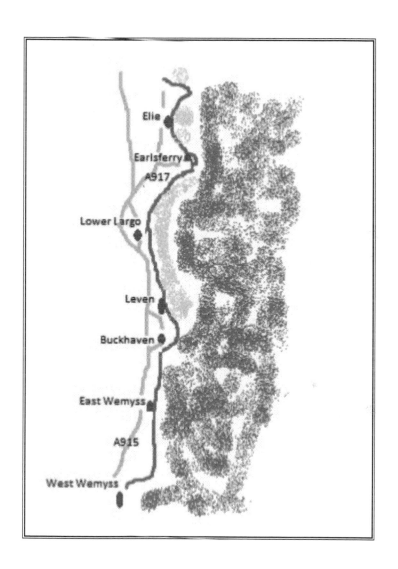

Why? Mainly because of the lovely wee cafe The Walk Inn, already described previously, where we could warm up before the return journey.

It was a bright January day, fresh with a sea breeze in our faces, so our stroll to West Wemyss was pleasant although uneventful. Then we enjoyed a light lunch of freshly prepared Cullen Skink, a local treat of haddock and potato soup, which we were now quite partial to. We were more observant on our return to East Wemyss, pausing beside castle walls of times gone by, with mysterious caverns beneath. I'd read that West Wemyss Castle gardens were not open to the public until April - a delight I would look forward to in the spring, being a lover of both gardens and gardening. Thinking of my plot down south I knew that I had not achieved anything spectacular - just a pleasurable space to lift my spirits. It's hard to juggle the demands of writing with a time consuming garden though, but soon I was to learn of a different way. The Kinghorn Way!

I lifted my camera to take a shot of the castle - difficult because it was set back in the shadows of ancient trees. When I peered at the view-finder, though, the trees had vanished and an impressive sandstone palatial home filled the tiny screen.

'That must have been quite something,' I spoke out loud.

'It is,' replied a stranger with a black top hat, cravat and a dark beige waistcoat - his boots almost up to the knees of his breeches. 'Enter,' he commanded as he held open a large wooden door set in the walls. I stepped past him and went inside without a backward glance. 'The name's Walter Nicol.'

He held out his hand to me but when I put my hand in his he lifted it to his lips and kissed it - a gesture which took me completely by surprise. 'Would you like me te show ye arund?'

'Oh, yes please. That would be wonderful.'

We walked around the gardens, beautifully laid out in curves and circles, with perfectly trimmed hedges and manicured lawns.

'This is my pride and joy,' he said as we entered a walled garden with all manner of fruit trees, bare of course at this time of year.

'This must be glorious in the summer,' I said.

'Alas I find myself out of employment this spring. My master thinks my plans are too lavish.'

'Tell me about your plans,' I said as we sat on a wooden bench in a sun drenched corner, where you'd think that spring had already arrived.

'I had hoped to have fruit for every month of the year with which my master could impress his guests.'

'What a lovely idea and so do you mind me asking what went wrong?'

'Money. It's as simple as that, lass. My master sells coal which is in abundance beneath our feet but the garden would cost the likes of one hundred tons of coal per year.'

'Phew, I see.'

'And so, after all this work - making all this beauty - I am out of a job.' Walter's downcast look reminded me of myself back in the spring of last year. Was it really so little time ago?

'I was made redundant too last spring but life is fine now. I wish I had the time and energy to make my own garden as special as this.'

'And the money.'

The irony of his reply was not lost on me.

'You have a gift with plants and such vision. You'll find another job. I'm sure of it.'

'Do you think so? If that's the case then I'm much encouraged by our chance encounter and I thank ye for it.'

'Surely it is I who must thank **you.** It has been a pleasure to be shown around your garden!'

My new friend bowed to me, flamboyantly sweeping his hat in front of him as he did so.

As I walked back through the gate and on to the path, the castle was now ancient and dark once more. I turned to wave but of course my companion had vanished.

'Time, money and inclination,' I must have spoken aloud again.

'What did you say?' asked my husband, who had walked a little further on whilst I was day dreaming.

'Time, money and inclination. That's what you always need to succeed and you rarely have all three at the same time, do you?'

'Oh I don't know. You have time and inclination to write novels and we have enough money at the moment. What more do you want? Come on, it will be getting dark before we get back to the car at East Wemyss if we're not careful.'

As I was walking back, as well as admiring the astonishing sunset, I was thinking of my garden back home in

Bedfordshire. On my visits home I have tried to keep it tidy - weed the beds, mulch them with last year's leaf mould and sweep up this year's leaves. It's as if it is frozen in a moment in time but what I couldn't do was to plan for the future. The woodland bed could have done with some more snowdrops and hellebores and the top bed needed a total replant, but it was impossible to either order or buy plants. Could I devote enough time to both my garden and my writing, I wondered? Niggled by a moment of flickering frustration I shook myself free, filling my lungs with the bracing sea air. It didn't really matter at that moment in time, did it?

I just had to let go of my garden in my mind, body and soul. When I was down in Bedfordshire I raced around trying to do everything, but achieved satisfaction with very little. Life was so much calmer in Fife and I felt at peace knowing what my priorities were.

Some might argue that we had shirked our responsibilities, coming away and living the dream, but it was only in leaving it all behind that we gained a clearer perspective of our lives.

As my thoughts were wandering I must confess to missing some of the scenery along this route. It's all a bit vague - a stony shoreline, a woodland path behind some small working yards then back into the village of East Wemyss. We'd seen the famous caves along the way too, but I'm assured that there were more impressive ones to come on our next walk out of East Wemyss and so I looked forward to that. I smiled as I glanced back towards the wind turbine in the distance. It was certainly visible today.

A couple of nights later I attended a 'Kinghorn-in-Bloom' meeting. I really hope the ladies and gents do not mind me mentioning them but, since we arrived in Kinghorn I had noticed that there were many driving forces which determined the ebb and flow of community life - The Lifeboat Station Crew and volunteers being one major factor. The Community Centre and church also play their part, along with a plethora of groups including The Historical Society and Kinghorn in Bloom.

I was thrilled to hear the news that Kinghorn-in-Bloom had won a well deserved Gold last year (2013 to 2016 to date) in Fife. I'd admired their cascading peach begonias, hanging baskets and tubs along the High Street and beds of perennials by the Carousel. There was also a wildflower garden down by the harbour, old rowing boats overflowing with colour in several locations and not forgetting the charming mosaics at Pettycur Harbour too - all enhancing the environment, making the Royal Burgh of Kinghorn a delight.

As I listened to the debates on colour themes and other far more ambitious projects, their enthusiasm and obvious joy in moments of inspiration, however outlandish at times, was infectious on that rainy January night. I was certain that this small band of big-hearted volunteers would achieve great things.

As I walked back 'home' I mused that, if I was living in Kinghorn more permanently, I could adopt a plot in the village and put my energy each week into a wee area that the whole community could enjoy - a manageable portion of Kinghorn to keep beautiful, rather than spend hours for my own pleasure. It was certainly food for thought.

My journal entry that night was:

Kinghorn Community Events are Thriving

Kinghorn revived its Village Show back in 2010 and has gone from strength to strength ever since, with its annual Scarecrow Competition gaining fame and frivolity throughout the region. The annual Spooky Walk staged by the Lifeboat Station volunteers continues to haunt both young and old alike. Black Rock Race and Kinghorn Gala are enjoyed by participants and onlookers alike.

The highlight of the year though, has to be the Christmas and New year festivities. There's Carol singing outside the church hall leading up to turning on the Christmas lights in the High Street, followed by a Santa's Sleigh ride through the streets of Kinghorn. This is followed on its heels by The Loony Dooks on New Year's Day, when fancy dressed locals take a dip in the sea, witnessed by merry-makers not brave enough to take the plunge - a truly remarkable sight.

CHAPTER 16

East Wemyss

Incognito

SOMETHING STRANGE HAPPENED two days later. We watched with interest as a platform structure was pulled by pilot boats up the Forth, but at one point it seemed to get stuck right opposite us, in the centre of our line of vision. Richard suggested that it could be waiting for high tide or that it might be stranded on a sand bank but later that night, when it lit up like a Christmas Tree and the tug and pilot boats vanished, I wasn't so sure. I hoped it wasn't a permanent feature or that they were searching for oil or something. You heard so many rumours.

'Don't worry,' said a friend in the village. 'It's come from the North Sea for some maintenance work to be carried out from Burntisland. They'll pull it back in due course.'

Although reassured somewhat I'm afraid this did not totally dispel my disquiet. The next morning it was misty and the offending structure had almost disappeared from view, along with the opposite shoreline, but I still knew it was there. It was like an unwanted blemish and my eyes were drawn to its shadow.

Needing a distraction I decided to pack a few things in my little rucksack and return to East Wemyss. I'd been intrigued by historical accounts of caves along the coastline which have sheltered many an inhabitant and visitor over the centuries, including smugglers and monks, kings and saints and I was keen to revisit the spot on my own. The first rocky cavern was not far from a parking bay at the sea front and a plaque explained that some early cave dwellers had left their mark inside - cave paintings which give a remarkable pictorial representation of the occupants and their lives. I walked along the path at the edge of the sea looking at the entrance to each cave, stroking the rock-face and wondering about the folks who dwelt there or who had sought refuge. I was drawn to an awareness of the endurance of rock, like ancient trees, they survive through the ages of man, witnessing unique events - moments in time. Rocks even hold many secrets of time even before man walked this earth - great eras in the history of the world. Suddenly my hands felt a vibration - an echo of past mining below perhaps, running footsteps within the depths of the cave, an earth tremor or maybe falling rocks.

Whatever the reason, I did not wait to find out but snapped out of my meditation. I rushed further along the already familiar path, away from the rocks - the sound of the sea and smell of the breeze calming my breath. The path bore inland and then up steep well hewn steps, until I reached the castle on the brow of the hill, stanzas of Macbeth haunting my every step. Once out in the open again I followed the old railway path to Newhaven, where I paused to eat my sandwiches on a bench on the cliff tops looking back along the coast to East Wemyss.

To my left the wind turbine, now visibly huge, prompted me to consider the platform which had encouraged me to take flight that morning - progress versus landscape protection, environmental considerations versus the need for industry and employment. I was momentarily filled with gratitude for the small pockets of industry dotted along the coast of Fife and I knew that the platform would irritate me no more.

Realising the implications of limited daylight, I began to walk back, taking photos of the caves as I passed them by. I could just see my car in the distance when a cloaked man approached me, his shadowy features virtually hidden beneath his hood. I had no way of avoiding him but before we met there was a noise from the cave to my left - the one I'd rushed away from earlier.

Two men sprang out with daggers pointing at us and we were both forced inside, shoved down on to the sandy floor and my bag was torn from my shoulders. Robbers, I thought, but glancing over to where the old man lay I noticed that he seemed to have nothing of worth to steal.

One of our assailants, an unshaven man with a scar over his right eye, looked on with disdain as another a dark lanky haired youth with smooth skin, pulled out the cling-film that had once held my sandwiches and an empty orange juice carton - my waterproof leggings, the most precious procession I had on my person, were thankfully unnoticed.

Suddenly the older man with the menacing face thrust his dagger towards us, his partner following suit, at which point my new companion, whom I'd not really had time to study, whipped off his cloak to reveal his kingly garb beneath.

Well. To my surprise the demeanour of both men changed dramatically as they bowed low in respect and grovelled apologetically. Next they offered us wine and chunks of grubby bread, which I dared not refuse, before letting us on our way. It was now dark and I was so relieved to be rushing back towards my car. I'd certainly had enough excitement that foggy night but I did glance over my shoulder thinking I might have a chance to thank my saviour, only to see him striding in the opposite direction. That evening I recorded:

The Legend of King James V lives on

It was said that King James V often went incognito around his kingdom and was once at East Wemyss. Set upon by robbers near a cave and dragged inside they threatened to kill him but at that moment he revealed his true identity. So respectful were the Fife folk of their king that they begged for pardon and he went on his way. The legend of the Guideman o'Ballengeich lives on and he is sometimes referred to as the poor man's king.

My plight, although disturbing at the time, did seem to answer one of my dilemmas. I could certainly have fun on Twitter and Facebook if I went on the internet incognito and make up a 'Nom de plume.' Just a thought.

I glanced out of the window. It was dark but the Christmas tree-like lights were glowing in the bay. I smiled.

CHAPTER 17

Leven to Lower Largo

No Person is an Island

THE FIRTH OF FORTH has a magnetic pull equally as powerful as the sea. There were times whilst living above Pettycur when I was deep in concentration, but I'd be drawn by an invisible force to put on my wellingtons and go down to the beach. One morning I could see from my vantage point that there was no-one about, possibly because it was high tide. I know that people had explained the difference between neap and spring tides, low-low tides and high-high tides, but it was not until we were living with the seas rhythm each day that I truly understood.

I walked along the foam where it caressed the shore-line, and I found a spot on the rocks to rest, looking over towards the harbour and the diffused sunlight. I settled my mind by praying with waves, like my elderly friend Fred had taught me to do years ago, naming each person important in my life with each wave, much like a mantra.

Family members first:

'Mum,' breathe 'Dad,' breathe, 'Richard,' breathe,Tom,' breathe, 'Joanna,' breathe, 'Alex', breathe, 'Carol,' breath ... I continued to my friends and other people I held dear. Not one white horse reached me as I offered each of these extra-special people to the sea and the elements. Names exhausted, I was just breathing, in and out, in and out. I could sense a stillness - my breath in total harmony with the waves.

As I came out of my reverie I strolled back through the shallows, becoming as one with each person for the greater good, and I was overwhelmed by how precious these moments were to me - just 'to be'. I would surely treasure them. I could so easily have missed this opportunity and chosen to continue to be busy believing that I didn't deserve a break. This thought led me perfectly to my next tale and the next stage in my journey along the Fife coastal path.

Yesterday it was my husband's day off and so we drove to Leven, pronounced *Leeven,* I think. We parked beside the beach, donned our walking boots and followed the coastal road a short distance before joining the beach. The tide was low enough to do virtually the whole walk along the sand. It was a lovely day. How could we be so blessed in the middle of February? We walked companionably, side by side, as the long bay curved towards villages in the distance, a steady walk on firm sand with the sun shining on our backs. It was less than three miles - a gentle wee stroll - but our aim was also to enjoy lunch in the Crusoe Hotel at Lower Largo, a place we'd loved on our first visit to Fife back in May. The village is one of those unspoilt places where you are aware of the wild rugged sea meeting the edge of the urban area of Leven in a most unexpected and pleasurable way.

Towards the end of the bay, accessible at mid tide, we veered inland taking the path across the golf course and through the scrubland tracks into the village itself. This crossed a bridge before reaching the hotel. To our left tiny cottages lined the river's edge as it headed out to sea. We not only enjoyed a hearty winter's meal but also lapped up the history of various mariners including the local man Alexander Selkirk, who inspired Daniel Defoe to write Robinson Crusoe.

The story goes that Alexander Selkirk disobeyed his parents by venturing on a life at sea at a very young age and ended up shipwrecked on an island in the South Pacific. A hand written version of his story is framed and hangs on the restaurant wall amongst other naval memorabilia.

Feeling replete after our wholesome lunch we strolled along the cobbled streets of fishermen's cottages, with their tiny doors, passing an unusual totem pole on the seaward side. Our destination, the monument of Alexander Selkirk, stands proudly at first floor level on a house wall not much further along the street. He wears the dishevelled garb of a castaway, as he gazes over his native homeland out to sea, a rifle at his side.

The moment I had taken the photo I was aware of this renowned sailor's presence beckoning me down to the harbour, where a single masted schooner was awaiting us. I should have asked him where the vessel had come from. It was certainly full of coal, so maybe this was an unscheduled stop from Dysart or Wemyss. Ever trustful of my guides, I followed Alexander up the gang plank. Although his garb was more civil than that of his statue, I was in no doubt as to his identity. We sailed for over an hour until we reached the most easterly island in the Firth of Forth, the Isle of May, where the men began to unload tons of coal. Alexander caught my attention by a flick of his head and an imperceptible raise of his left hand, leading me away from the harbour. We walked over the island along a track to a well above a cliff, with sea stacks down to a rocky inlet. I was so lost in my thoughts that I flinched as my guide handed me some water and began to speak.

'That bay is called Pilgrim's Haven and here's a drop of courage for you from Pilgrim's Well. You are certainly going to need it on the next leg of your pilgrimage. I can assure you that you will never be marooned on a deserted island like I was but you **will,** almost certainly, enjoy your solitude. When you feel lonely, and you surely will at times, your salvation will be to reach out and give of yourself to others. I know that there will be opportunities aplenty. Your destiny is to achieve great things if you follow your course wisely.'

However many questions I asked after he had finished speaking, nothing could cajole my companion to say anymore and so I drank the proffered cup and followed him back to the ship, lost in my own space, thinking on his words. I'd never considered my journey as a pilgrimage up until that point, but the more I considered it, the more apt I felt that description to be - especially if I achieved my goal of walking virtually from Dunfermline to St Andrew's along the coast. How many footsteps of pilgrims would I tread in? How many life changing moments would I live, breath, sleep and walk along on the way? What lessons would I learn from those I meet? Why would I need courage and what would I achieve? As we sailed back to Lower Largo I dwelt on these things. I had far more questions than answers. Occasionally I glanced over to Alexander but he neither caught my eye nor said another word.

After walking back along the jetty near The Crusoe I turned, but neither the ship nor my silent companion were to be seen. I made my way to the bench at the bus stop, under the shelter of the disused viaduct and was not surprised to find my husband waiting for me. Taking the seat at the front on the top of the double-decker, a childhood pleasure revisited, we felt a part of the changing landscape as we headed back to Leven. We chatted about Lower Largo, our walk and the meal we'd enjoyed. I did not mention my meeting with Andrew Selkirk. Best not to!

That night I recorded in my journal:

Two facts you may not know about Daniel Defoe, the writer of Robinson Crusoe, was that he was a spy, amongst other literary occupations. The phrase 'English Novel' was also thought to be used for the first time when Robinson Crusoe was first published in 1719. The 'novel' was based on the life of a true Fifer, called Alexander Selkirk who was stranded on an island in the Pacific for four years. Undeterred by this experience, the real Alexander spent a lifetime at sea.

CHAPTER 18

Back in Bedfordshire

Listen to the heartbeat of 'home'

DRIVING DOWN SOUTH to Bedfordshire the following weekend was the antithesis of my original journey to Scotland the previous August. I felt the passing of each mile as if I was leaving something precious behind; the constantly changing scenery from wild and rugged to gentle and rolling and finally to almost flat as I passed from county to county - from unspoilt to densely populated - from relatively quiet roads to traffic jams. Back then, in August, it was beautiful sunshine when I reached the coast above Berwick, aware of the Fife coastline across the water, drawing me to my destination. This time it was pouring with rain. The seas were raging as I passed Berwick and at the A1 roundabout my Sat Nav announced *'keep on one hundred and fourteen miles before reaching the next turn'* - an endless stretch of road towards, dare I call it, 'home'.

I thought little on the journey, pausing for three short fifteen minute comfort stops. Was it my imagination or were drivers less courteous the further south I travelled. If they saw that I was trapped behind a vehicle and wanted to get into the middle lane, instead of flashing me out or moving over, as they tended to do in Scotland, they rushed past as if to say, 'got you!' Everyone was in too much of a hurry. The stress of the south began to weigh on me.

I was glad I'd brought a filled roll and orange juice cartons, to avoid the £3.75 for a Latté. I'd also thought that a full tank of diesel would get me back but I'd just passed the services in Lincolnshire when I noticed that I was heading towards the red. It was Sunday and services were few but, whereas my old self would have fretted, I reasoned that I would reach Peterborough well in time. I relaxed, adjusting my speed to just over 65 to conserve fuel. I made it – just in time.

It was after Peterborough that the sun skimmed the horizon. A glorious sky was illuminating an otherwise empty landscape, devoid of hills. I could not help but wonder if it was really the same sky which we gazed upon at Pettycur. Strangely, I received a text message from Richard later that evening about the sunset - a feeling of togetherness that we should be witnessing the same beauty so many miles apart.

I drove along the back roads for the final few miles, the twilight giving just enough light to make driving easy. *Shepherd's View* stood, just as it did when I left in December, and as I walked inside I was struck by how nothing had actually changed. The house had waited - perfectly - silently. I turned up the heating and thrust open all the doors to air the rooms. Then I stood listening. It wasn't quite the reassurance of a beloved pet, smothering me with affection, but it was more like a brooding step child - timid in the loneliness it was reluctant to shed, just in case. In case of what?

Eight years ago, when we moved into *Shepherd's View*, I loved the place unreservedly. It was potentially beautiful with a neglected charm. (My husband would not have described it quite like that!) It was certainly warm and welcoming. The previous owners had showered *Shepherd's View* with affection in their own way. As we agreed to buy it the lady remarked,

'I'm so glad to see that you will love *Shepherd's View* as much as we have.'

Nevertheless it was in a bit of a time warp with very few obvious improvements since the 1970's, so renovating it became a project for us. We planned to take five years but in the end it took more like seven. With each update - new boiler, electric re-wiring, tired built in cupboards to pull down, layers of wallpaper on walls and ceilings to strip and plaster to mend, *Shepherd's View* groaned, protested and fought back. The house didn't enjoy it one bit and made sure we didn't either. It was strange though; once each stage was completed the whole home seemed to sigh with relief, even with a hint of approval - almost with embarrassment that she'd made so much fuss in the first place.

Nevertheless I loved her throughout the painful experience, but it was a sad day when realisation dawned on me that Richard didn't feel quite the same way. At times he saw her as a chain around his neck and to Bedfordshire; a drain of his money and resources. Whereas I longed to settle and to establish firm roots, Richard wanted to be uprooted and to travel - to visit exotic places.

'It's OK for you. You've seen the world,' he'd say.

'Not all of it,' I'd say, and so it would go on.

So now, sitting here in the quiet, and yes *Shepherd's View* is certainly quiet, I can almost hear her asking,

'Do you still love me? When are you coming 'home'?'

I believe that a place has a heart, and this one is still beating, albeit faintly, wondering what we will do next.

'How could I think to leave you?' I say, but the reality is that I am already torn in two.

Ode to Shepherd's View
In a dip on the hillside
You hide from view
Unseen by passersby.
Your quietness stills the aching soul
I can sense you heave a sigh.
To be cherished is all your heart desires
To be filled with laughter and love
Who knows if I'll see you to my life's end?
Only Him above.

CHAPTER 19

LowerLargo to Elie

Your Fears are your Greatest Foes

THREE DAYS LATER I was back in Kinghorn after a frenzy of activity down south, visiting family and friends, catching up with members of my writers' group and working on tidying another corner of the garden. It was a weekend in mid February and we were on the trail again.

Donning two layers of coats, gloves and my trademark pink woolly hat we left our car at Lower Largo, retracing our steps in the winter sunshine towards Alexander's monument. I paused to smile up at him, recalling his every word of warning but also his encouragement. At the edge of the village, from a small car park, the coastal path veered up steps to follow the course of another old railway line above the bay, once used to shift coal. The tide was out and so, after about half a mile, we decided to slip down through the grassy sand dunes and back on to the beach. This enabled us to quicken our pace, aware of dark clouds following us from behind and another nearly eight miles of unknown territory ahead of us. You may find my descriptions of weather hard to believe. After all we were experiencing winter on the east coast of Scotland, but we were learning to check hourly weather reports on the Internet just before setting out and would plan our trips accordingly - whether an early morning start was best or to wait until nearer lunchtime, or not to venture out at all. Yes, there were days like that too, but on the whole the weather was kind to us and we felt blessed to be spending so much time enjoying the pleasures of outdoors throughout the year.

At first we met a few people strolling with their dogs along the flat sands, veering around large black boulders. We nearly missed the footpath sign in the dunes above us as we neared the estuary, the beach now deserted. This path led us through Dunbarnie Links Wildlife Reserve, across numerous wooden walkways and bridges, which took us safely over to the other side of this marshy terrain and rushing river.

We headed for a gap in the tree line, through which there was an expanse of deserted caravans where the coastal path joined one of the tracks of Elie Caravan Park - eerie in its out of season state. We continued, pausing to sit a few moments overlooking Shell Bay, a picturesque beach leading to the cliff ahead of us.

It was at the extremities of this sandy bay that the terrain changed markedly. On the one hand the dark forbidding rocks clung to the cliff face as the stretch of beach narrowed to craggy inlets and pool filled outcrops. Alternatively there was the more welcoming rocky path which ambled ever upwards, away from the beach and up the cliff to the top.

I stopped to take a photo but this time it was as if my split personality cloned into two individuals. Through the viewfinder I watched as I disappeared from view, like a large red mountain goat with a pink woolly hat, my husband following close behind. My other self took a lower path to the edge of the overhang. Here I paused to take a photo of the bay from whence we'd come and when I looked up my new guide was standing beside me, gazing out to the horizon. He was a tall grey haired man, light complexion and clean-shaven with piercing blue-brown eyes which peered at me from under his red safety helmet.

'This way,' my guide said as he proffered an identical helmet for me to put on, its ominous presence filling me with foreboding, Alexander's words echoing in my head. He waited patiently while I tied the strap under my chin, my fingers fumbling with fear and then he seemed to disappear over the cliff. I peered down after him.

'I hope you don't think I'm going to follow you,' I called softly. 'I'm afraid of heights.'

'I believe you have more serious fears to shed than acrophobia. You'll be fine.'

I had no choice but to follow the man and I flinched, my whole body tense as I left the comfort of the grassy bank above. After a while, though, I was concentrating so much on finding footholds and clinging to the vertical chain hanging down in front of me that I barely noticed the drop, and soon I was safely down on horizontal, well almost terra-firma, rocks below. Exhilarated by my achievement I grinned.

'This is a *"can do"* and not a *"no can do"* walk Diana. Well done, you've passed the first test but we've got a long way to go. There are eight chains in all but concentrate on one at a time and you'll be fine.'

I tried to ignore the growing fear inside me as we walked over a stony inlet passing Devil's Cave. I shuddered.

'Come along,' my guide said. 'We need to beat the tide. Keep your eyes on where you are going and concentrate on what you are doing, but don't allow yourself to look down,' then he turned from me.

At first I followed him quite easily, reaching a horizontal chain with a ledge for our feet. I was beginning to feel quite confident and pleased with myself until we reached the third chain, which clung to the cliff. Once again my hands were sweating, as salty as the sea.

'Take care of loose stones,' my guide called back, too late! I had slipped and I clung to the chain, whilst one foot hung precariously in thin air. Within moments he was by my side holding me. I could feel his strength, calming and secure. My body stilled as my wayward foot found firmness underneath. As I relaxed, so did his hold of me. Are you OK? his eyes asked.

'You're bound to stumble from time to time but trust in your own strength and believe in yourself and you will succeed.'

As I continued upwards, occasionally I felt my footing slither, but if I paused a moment, took a deep breath and focussed on my goal I found I could move forward, slowly but surely. It was a long ascent, and steep at times. I strained, all muscles in my body alert, whilst my guide stood at the top on a knife edge ridge admiring the view. With relief I reached him but was unable to stand. Instead I was content to sit on this ridge beside his feet. With sheer relief I closed my eyes.

'You're just not good enough,' a voice inside me said. 'You're just an amateur,' another clamoured at my diving sense of self worth. 'Who do you think you are?' came a further put down.

'You're letting your doubts and fears shadow your whole being just as the cloud has momentarily covered the sun. Clouds pass, but you are the same person whether in darkness or in light. When you can feel the rays of the sun on your face once more, open your eyes and stand with me and I promise that you will not be disappointed.'

A few moments passed but soon I felt the sun warming my cheeks and could hear the steady sound of the waves on the rocks below. I opened my eyes to see my guide's outstretched hand and without a second thought I took it. I breathed deeply and stood up, gazing out over the rocks below and the expanse of rippling sea. It was fantastic. Exhilarating. Amazing. Wonderful.

The chain down to the next inlet was not nearly so challenging; either that or I had already overcome so many of my hidden fears that I did not let them concern me, but nevertheless it was a relief to feel the sand and stones beneath my feet again. Unfortunately my peace was short lived. My most challenging chain was before me, vertical and at first it was almost impossible to find a footing. I gritted my teeth, this time forbidding any of my demons to reappear.

'I can do it,' I spoke aloud, as I clung to the chain, keeping it between my legs. My ascent was painfully slow, but I was certainly making progress, so much so that I was jubilant to reach the metal post above!

'You certainly can,' grinned my guide as he led me across steps carved in the rocks, springing down from ledge to ledge. He paused at a narrow gap between the rock faces of the cliff.

'I'm not going to do that,' I said flatly as I watched my companion grab the sixth chain to guide himself over a gap between cliff faces,' but his eyes encouraged otherwise.

I looked over my shoulder and in my imagination I retraced all the trials I had over-come. I sighed and gazed around me. There was no going back. In that split second I thought of all the times in my life I'd ducked out of a challenge, thrown by what I felt were insurmountable problems and perceived failure or by what people had said and I had searched for an easy way out. I had listened to those nagging voices and my whole being had longed, screamed out even, to give up. Then, often at the last moment, I had found some steely strength, making a last determined effort, and yes, I had succeeded. What now? In those seconds I felt my whole past stretch out before me like the ocean, whereas the steps to my future success were on the rock face ahead of me with only a gaping ravine in between.

I reached out for the chain and took that step of a life-time and do you know what? It felt fantastic!

The tide was out and so we were able to scramble over the shingle and rocks before locating the seventh chain. This one took us along the cliff face, with a ledge for our feet. It led to the famous Macduff's Cave. I had no desire to linger here or meet Macduff, and anyway my guide had only paused a moment or two before reaching for our last chain and the short descent to the rocks and the end of my Fife Chain Walk - a life-changing experience.

There was no need for my guide to stress the lessons I had learnt about myself whilst in his care before he bid me farewell, pointing towards a steep cliff face of steps.

'Go and join up with your other half,' he said, his eyes shining. 'From there you will be able to look back and see the path you have already travelled. Each time you stumble, and you will, or your inner fears surface, replay that leap in your imagination. With renewed confidence and faith in yourself, you will relax and enjoy your chosen path in life and experience the full satisfaction of moments of success. But remember Diana, never be complacent. A new challenge will invariably appear following each moment of sheer joy. Have courage!

I thanked my guide before racing up the steps. There must have been at least a hundred of them but when I reached the top I was laughing so much I had the stitch and needed to pause a moment to catch breathe. When I straightened I could see my other self laughing too. I walked towards the bench where she and my husband were sitting and we gazed out to sea together, across towards Pettycur Bay on the distant horizon. As we sat, we smiled, and as we smiled we merged back into one.

'We've walked all that way,' I said aloud, unable to hide the incredulity in my voice.

'We did it,' my other self echoed in the breeze.

The dark clouds had miraculously vanished and it was so warm that I took off my outer coat and breathed in the beautiful air.

'It's been a lovely walk,' said Richard.

'Wonderful,' I replied, truly whole.

After a short break we walked down the steps on the other side of the cliff, taking the path beside the golf course. It was a special moment as we reached the peninsula at Earlsferry, the point where the coast begins to point westwards and we lose sight of Kinghorn on the other side of the bay.

We ambled wearily through the tiny streets of Earlsferry and I was so relieved to reach a cafe in Elie. We had just enough time for a sandwich of smoked salmon and prawns before catching the bus back to Lower Largo - the eight mile stretch of our pilgrimage along the coastal path complete. But was I, I pondered, complete?

The Elie Chain Walk in Fife is said to have been constructed in the 1920's. There are eight chains altogether which take you half a kilometre from Shell Bay, around the cliff face to the golf course at Earlsferry. It can take up to 3 hours and although checked for safety by engineers it is both hazardous and strenuous. A good level of fitness and appropriate footwear and clothing is essential, as is a good knowledge of the tides.

A ferry used to link North Berwick with Earlsferry and in 1054 Macduff, the Earl of Fife, was said to have escaped from King Macbeth this way, aided by a local fisherman. By the 12th century it was the main route for pilgrims travelling from Holy Island in Northumberland to St Andrews in Fife.

A helpful guide to the chain walk is on <u>James Carron.wordpress</u>

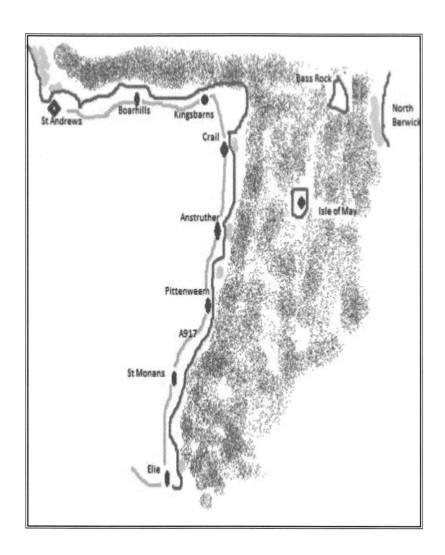

CHAPTER 20

Elie to Pittenweem

Sinners and saints

I LIKE ELIE. It has an air of affluence - a deli and coffee shops to lure your senses with anticipation and a traditional oak beamed public house overlooking the harbour, The Ship Inn, where people flock in the summer months.

(The Ship Inn has recently been renovated so I'm told)

A built up slip road shelters the harbour and the long narrow strip of sand from Elie to Earlsferry. In contrast, on the other side of these sea defences, the natural beauty of seaweed strewn rocks and a sandy cove, interestingly called Wood Haven, leads the eye towards the lighthouse, an important landmark along this coastline. People say that, if you are lucky enough, you might find a ruby rock, garnets really, if you scour the area below the lighthouse on your way to Ruby Bay.

I refrained from taking a photo of the little bathing hut below the lighthouse, allegedly used by Lady Anstruther for bathing around 1760. However sunny it was on that February morning, my skin felt numb with cold at the thought of joining her ladyship for a swim. Not that she would have appreciated my company. Apparently the village folk were warned to keep well away to protect the lady's modesty.

On the day we chose to go to Elie it was tranquil. My husband was tired after his working week so I continued this section of the walk on my own. The amble from Elie to St Monans was pleasant and yet uneventful, following the path amongst the grassy dunes above the bay passing two ancient castles. The path takes a trail between the remaining walls of Ardros Castle, whereas the ruins of Newark Castle still towers on the cliff's edge. At this point I had two choices. At high tide an alternative path crosses farmland and into the back of St Monans but I was fortunate to be able to take the coastal route. My final strides were steps cut out of the rocks just in front of the wee Kirk of St Monans. I had to leap across a couple of ever growing pools of water as the tide reclaimed the path. In fact, when I looked back, the steps had virtually disappeared. Foolhardy or fortunate - I was not quite sure which.

I ambled among the stone cottages and fishing harbour, ignorant of the passing of the ages, a perfect setting for a costume drama, maybe, from the days when the industries of fishing, salt and coal were at their peak.

(In fact much of Outlander was filmed in this region of Fife)

The next landmark of note, just outside St Monans on the farthest side above the harbour, was the restored windmill, below which were the remains of saltpans where surplus and low quality coal was used to heat the sea water to extract salt. It is difficult today to imagine a time when salt was seen as a precious commodity which we exported extensively.

The following coastline was wild, adorned with rock pools teeming with life, and the uplifting sound of white winged gulls and grebes competing with the sea. I stood and gazed towards the Isle of May and Bass Rock - a pointed white tooth piercing the sea, the sun-light reflecting the largest northern gannet colony in the world, which we'd once seen on webcams in the Scottish Seabird Centre at North Berwick over the water. Glancing down to the shore there was a pre World War One salt water swimming pool, occupied more often these days by prawns and crabs than people, especially in February. Within moments I was walking through the pretty village of Pittenweem, one of the centres of Fife fishing even today - a deceptive village in size. I was compelled to do a detour off the coastal path and up Cove Wynd to visit St Fillan's Cave, the entrance of which is sealed off from the public by a white cross, crafted into a locked gate. I took a photo.

Sure enough, as I returned my camera to its case, the gate creaked open for me to pass through and an old hooded monk sat in its darkness. He motioned for me to sit on a rocky shelf opposite him and his penetrating grey eyes observed me for a while in silence, peering from under his hood along his long bony nose-line, his countenance quite daunting. Finally, in a quiet but commanding voice he spoke,

'You are nearing the end of your journey my daughter. You have come so far and learnt much but you have one more major lesson before you reach St Andrews and your goal,' His expression softened into almost a smile.

I waited.

'I am Fillan. You will read of me as a saint but no one is perfect,' he chuckled. 'My only vice is not taking life seriously enough ... but you ... you are the very opposite. In order to be fulfilled on this pilgrimage, you need to leave something of yourself here in my cave.'

Finally I found my voice, 'but I have little in my rucksack I can give. What should I leave with you?'

The man smiled and his lined face filled with light. 'You'll know,' he said and he left me to my solitude - my mind blank. I must have sat there many minutes, maybe an hour, staring at the stone altar and Holy well, the focal points of the shrine. Nothing happened. He did not return.

I put my hands in my pockets to keep them warm, the chill of the shadows of the cave seeping into me. Feeling some tiny shells I had collected along the way, as a form of distraction I counted them - seven in all.

My dream of calling myself an author - I placed the smooth *Trough* shell on the altar, its orange and brown lines radiating like a bar code from its centre.

Self worth - I placed a matching pair of tiny *Branded Wedge* shells, their purple and yellow stripes like Hula Hoops of colour.

My gift of teaching – a *Grey Top* shell, its whorls spiralling from grey to bright white.

Letting go - a *Common Razor*, its curve long, sharp and decisive.

A balance between solitude and self giving - a *Common Cockle*, pure white and rough at the edges.

Trusting in my own strength - the sharply pointed spiralling *Auger* shell.

Then the last, a rough and ugly *Oyster* shell sat in the palm of my hand. I waited. The word 'success' filled me, but as soon as it entered the cavernous tunnels of my brain, self doubt crept back in along with conceit and pride fighting for place - my mind torn by indecision.

At that point Fillan reappeared from steps at the back of the cave. He took the shell and gently prised it open revealing the smooth mother of pearl interior and there in its centre was a tiny pearl. He placed the shell on top of my cairn and stood back.

'It's not a sin to succeed Diana,' and he held out his hands to me. I stood, placing my hands in his, feeling his warmth and strength fill my very being. As he let go I felt the tiny pearl in the palm of my left and writing hand.

'You have pearl inside you. Believe in it.'

'Thank you so much,' I said, my eyes moist as his grey eyes smiled farewell.

Outside I found the sun dazzling, reflected off white stone walls. The bus was only a few minutes away and I mused on another glorious and thought provoking day as I headed the short distance back to Elie. I jotted in my notebook:

Facts about St Fillan

St Fillan, a missionary saint in the seventh century is alleged to have lived in the cave while he converted the local Picts to Christianity. Thus it is one of the oldest Christian religious sites in Scotland. The village name Pittenweem means 'town of the cave.'

My husband had enjoyed a coffee and a chat with the locals before taking a leisurely stroll around the harbour, where he'd found signs of volcanic activity in rock formation beside the old granary. Then he'd ambled to the Elie Deli to meet me for lunch. We ate some wholesome soup and a delicious chunk of seeded loaf before heading back from the East Neuk to Pettycur. The region of East Neuk certainly has its own charm. It is reminiscent of The Channel Islands and to Richard it reminded him of his beloved Cornwall. It is not surprising that we both felt so at home in Fife.

CHAPTER 21

Pittenweem to Anstruther to Crail

Honesty to those close by

IT WAS EARLY March and we were blessed by another sunny Wednesday so we headed back to East Neuk. We paused to try another flavour of scone in one of Elie's cafes – I had walnut and date and Richard enjoyed cheese and bacon – delicious! I marked them ten out of ten on my scone quality indicator, only equalled by a small cafe in Mullion Cove, Cornwall where they call them Splits instead.

Then we drove on to Pittenweem. There are two possible paths out of the village, the lower route along the shoreline, only to be attempted at low tide as in much of this stretch of coastal path, or alternatively across the fields and along the cliff top. We chose the lower route, which follows a stony path, passing another rock bathing pool and then rising on to a grassy point called Billow Ness. It is here that the coast turns and we paused to enjoy the view of Anstruther, pronounced '*Ainster*', by the locals, ahead of us. Just off the rocks below us we could identify Johnny Doo's Pulpit where the famous local man practiced his sermons from 1780 to 1847. We did not pause to hear his haunting voice.

The grassy path turned to tarmac as we approached Anstruther Golf Clubhouse, protected by high fences - or were the barriers rather to prevent the balls from falling down the cliff and into the sea, we wondered. The path wove its way through the outskirts of Anstruther. The narrow street was quite busy so we were pleased to pause in The Dreel Tavern for a cold drink, an ancient pub which bears a plaque telling the story of a beggar woman who was rewarded by a purse of gold when she carried James V, the *guid man o' ballengeich*, over the burn.

'Don't sit there,' exclaimed the kindly barman, as I headed to the nearest table. He pointed to another sign above my head. 'That's George's seat, our resident ghost. This is the most haunted pub in Fife, you know.'

I shifted along to leave room for George.

'He switches the lights on and off sometimes,' the barman warmed to his age old tale. 'It used to be a brothel,' he said with a wink as he turned to serve another customer.

We laughed as we relaxed. It was not difficult to imagine the goings on in those dark corners of yesteryear. We were tempted to stay for lunch but another famous place in Anstruther beckoned. The fish and chip shop. Who could resist Anstruther haddock?

After a sharp bend we stopped to admire Buckie House, a building adorned with shells. Thankfully a bridge now crosses the burn after which we turned right, weaving our way down to the harbour. After browsing amongst the shops we relished the thought of our next stop as we queued for a table. The smell of freshly cooked local haddock teased our taste buds as we sipped our tea, but it was well worth the wait.

Satisfied and content we were ready for the next leg of our walk but first we ambled along the harbour arm, a perfect vantage point for views of both the town and the sea. We intended to take a closer look at the North Carr Lightship which once was stationed off Fife Ness. After taking several shots of Anstruther I jumped as I was tapped on the shoulder by young man of about my height, with a substantial moustache and hair bobbed around his ears, wearing a velveteen blazer jacket with silk trimmed lapels. He smiled.

'My father is working on this breakwater. If you could be so good as to move along to safety nearer the shore. The workmen will commence their labours soon.'

I looked down and instead of standing on a firm concrete pathway my feet were resting on a path of rubble and boulders, stretching out into the sea. He held out his hand and I grasped it.

'Robert Louis Stevenson at your service madam,' he said letting go of my hand once I was back on safer ground.

'Diana Jackson,' I replied smiling, 'and thank you.'

'Would you care to join me for breakfast?'

I glanced in surprise towards the sun which was now only just above the horizon.

'I would like that very much,' I replied, finding it hard to believe my good fortune to meet another famous author along this trail. I did not pause to think that it might look a trifle suspicious as I followed this young man along to his lodgings at Cunzie House. Once there Mrs Mac Donald made a place for me to join Mr Stevenson for a hearty bowl of Scottish porridge followed by smoked kipper. I found the saltiness of the former an acquired taste, but I resisted the temptation to cover it with lashings of sugar. Anyway, I could see none on the table.

'My father will expect me back down at the harbour in half an hour so my time is limited but I sense that you are a kindred spirit going through a similar struggle as myself.'

A little in awe of my young companion, I just nodded and smiled.

Mr Stevenson barely hesitated before continuing, 'My father wishes me to join him in his successful engineering business and to this end I have been studying in Edinburgh, though a trifle half-heartedly I must admit.'

'What do you truly wish to do with your life?' I asked, already guessing the answer.

He grinned with understanding. 'Every moment of the day I desire to write. All my senses inspire me to use language to effect. I so wish to travel and to live a bohemian life, unrestrained by the formality and precision of life as an engineer. I need to tell my parents and soon, but it is in this respect I find myself devoid of appropriate words - totally speechless.'

'I understand your dilemma, but I can also see that a career as an engineer would be as inappropriate for you as it would be for me. Having said that, being a writer will be no easy route for you to take either. You need to be sure. Once you are certain then you must be honest with those who love you and pray that they show understanding. Your father will suffer a huge disappointment and your mother will be filled with concern for you, but a life of an engineer should not be pursued lightly either. Can you imagine a surgeon entering his profession half-heartedly? How many would die under his clumsy knife? A writer's brain is wired completely differently to that of a scientist. I am not saying that a scientist cannot write, far from it, but each form of writing has its place, in the same way that each person has a way in life to follow and individual goals to pursue.'

'But I no longer think that I can even pray for guidance,' he continued, his smooth face showing frown lines of anguish. 'I'm not even sure whether I remain a believer.'

'Whether you have faith in God or not, you certainly perceive spirituality in nature and the world you write about. Send your pleas to the elements. If you are in earnest they will respond accordingly.'

'So what should I do?'

'Be honest with your parents at the first possible opportunity. You'll see. Both will find it difficult at first but they will adapt if they see your intentions are genuine.'

My companion's face relaxed, showing a resolve which overshadowed his former doubts. I could see a reflection of myself in his eyes.

Sensing this he said, 'You too are confused by your desire to write. I believe that although the way ahead is uncertain for you, and you have difficult decisions to make, your resolve to pursue a writing career is rock steady. It can be a lonely existence though, and you need to find a balance between fellowship and isolation in your life.' He paused. 'I must go now but I am grateful for this chance encounter.' He rose and taking my hand he kissed it before leading me to the door.

Once outside I was disorientated for a while, but walking back down to the harbour I could see Richard looking at the North Carr Lightship berthed in the outer harbour. The trip boats to the Isle of May were idly waiting for the season to begin and so we promised to return on a future date to visit both and also to spend some time at the Fisheries Museum.

Wanting to walk off our substantial lunch (and my extra breakfast too!) we pressed on, passing the tiny harbour of Cellardyke where we were amused to see that the enterprising residents had hung their washing in the shelter of the harbour walls. A small caravan site marked the edge of the Anstruthers, beside which ran our coastal path, an easy stroll betwixt fenced off farmland and the bay. At a kissing gate the terrain changed, crossing over a series of stepping stones before reaching a more uneven way of craggy rocks and gentle slopes, where dramatic outcrops towered over us in hues of orange, red and yellow. We decided not to follow the lure into Chapel Cave at this point, remembering the advice that it is better to do such things with a guide. Instead we continued on our way. A hilly grassland followed, at which point we spotted a line of large white sea birds far out at the water's edge. Delving in our rucksack for our binoculars we were surprised at the unusual sight of a flock of swans, maybe twenty or more resting in the shallows.

For the last half a mile out of Crail the inclines were more pronounced with a final ascent of steep steps at the top of which was a dip of grass. From there Crail Harbour came into view, a popular spot to feature on calendars and jigsaw puzzles, arguably the most beautiful in Fife. Our way down was via shallow wide steps winding their way among wee cottages.

After strolling around the harbour we found a cafe with a sheltered courtyard over-looking the sea where we enjoyed a cup of tea before a hail shower prompted us to move on and catch the bus back to Pittenweem and our car.

A Swashbuckling Tale from a Fine New Author - August 1883

Scottish writer Robert Louis Stevenson has gained well deserved success with his first book Treasure Island, recently published as a serial in the children's magazine 'Young Folks.' Long John Silver and his adventurous escapades will excite any boy in the land.

(Sad to say The Dreel Tavern has now closed. As their website says so eloquently, 'The Dreel Tavern has become a victim of our times.')

CHAPTER 22

Crail to Kingsbarns

Life is like a game of golf. Give it your best shot.

WE WERE AWARE that the remaining sections of our walk were going to be the longest and possibly the toughest stretches so far and so we stopped off at the now familiar Elie Deli to buy some pies and a couple of bottles of water for sustenance along the way. Once parked in Crail we had coffee in a small cafe called Julia's where we got into an interesting debate about Scottish independence.

We admired the harbour once more before following the track through a small caravan park and then along the grassy footpaths above the shoreline. For a long stretch we strolled along the sand avoiding seaweed and rocky outcrops and then along the sea's edge of Kilminning Coast Wildlife reserve. Occasionally, when protected from a fierce wind, we took off our fleeces, but most of the time an open jacket was all we needed in the spring sunshine.

After about two and a half miles we said goodbye to the misty view of the Borders and North Berwick across the estuary as we turned at the Coastguard Station of Fife Ness, a strange urban area in an otherwise rough coastline where a gun emplacement and other remnants of WW2 are still visible.

A small road took us behind the buildings and then back to the wilds beside the sea. This seemed a good moment to find a sheltered rocky ledge where we paused to eat our pies - all the more tasty laced with fresh air and the salt of the sea. Sitting back to back I gazed towards the deserted coastline ahead whereas Richard looked back towards Fife Ness. There were just the two of us, the sea birds and the elements. I felt at peace.

A good long drink of water and we were soon on our way, walking gingerly along the edge of the Crail Society golf course, the seventh oldest society in the world. We had one eye out for golfers and the other on the scenery – the greens stretching before us with sea and sand below.

It is not surprising that people love to play golf here, I thought, with this wonderful scenery. I took a photo of the sweep of the bay and then heard a cry.

'Fore.'

Although a few moments before the area had been completely deserted, an elderly white bearded gentleman had appeared and was about to tee off. His tweed jacket was just hiding a gold watch and chain which peaked from beneath his lapel - one button done up casually at his waist.

I froze in respect of his shot and watched in astonishment as the golf ball flew and landed on the green inches from the flag. He beckoned me over and in silence I walked with him and watched his final effortless putt into the hole.

'A birdie,' he said. 'I'm Tom Morris, but ye can call me Old Tom. Everyone else does.'

'Diana Jackson,' I replied.

''Come wi' me,' he said and so I walked beside him over the undulations of the course. 'I'm not just a golfer here, I'm the chief greenkeeper and it's been a pleasure over the years to improve this course. Look at those bunkers.' He pointed to areas where the grass dipped and each pit was filled with sand - the edges neatly trimmed. Again I was left speechless. I knew nothing about golf.

'When I came here those were rugged and unkempt - more like part of the rough and as each golfer had the misfortune to get their balls stuck, the worse they got.' He chuckled at the picture conjured by his memory. 'One of the first things I did 'ere was to tidy 'em up and to keep 'em that way.

We walked on along a gravel pathway from one fairway to the next.

'Making clear pathways made sure that the fairways were kept pristine and the grass protected too.'

He lifted his arm in a gesture of pride. 'We look after the grass grand. We feed it and nurture it, cutting it to precision. It's all about attention to detail and an element of love.'

'Do you enjoy your game all the more - knowing that the course is tended to with care?'

'Course I do. I only play for pleasure now and to teach the youngsters a thing or two, but I'll have ye know lassie that I've won four open championships in my day.'

I smiled, hoping I looked suitably impressed.

'What I'm trying to tell ye lassie is, don't accept anything less than perfection. Improve, improve, improve fer all yer life. Work at it and you'll feel satisfied yer've done yer best. That's what it's all aboot.'

He held out his bony hand and I shook it warmly.

'Thank you so much,' I said as he pointed to the path from whence we'd come.

Richard was standing looking out to sea. 'Maybe I'll take up golf when I retire,' he said, before we continued on our walk together.

The next section was a deceptively rough scramble along the coastline before arriving at a row of trees which marked the boundary of Kingsbarns Golf Course and Cambo Gardens, a place of perfect curves and shades of green which looked painted on the landscape, with its golfers charging around on motorised buggies - a far cry from my recent encounter.

This is the only place where we made an unofficial detour off our planned course as we lost the path and were lured by the gently undulating slopes of the tarmac golf course tracks. We should have continued along the coast here for another half a mile before walking through the village. Feeling like trespassers, obvious by our lack of equipment and the fact that we were actually walking, we strode purposefully to the grand boundary gate and entrance to the course. It was a further three quarters of a mile along to the main road until we finally reached the bus stop beside the church. Confused by the bus timetable, which seemed to tell us that there were no buses, we phoned the number given on the sign. The lady who spoke to me could not have been more helpful as she located our position from the number on the bus stop and reassured us that there would be a bus along in fifteen minutes. We waited contentedly in the sunshine, albeit a little foot-sore. The ride back was excellent yet again, reliving the sights of our walk from the different perspective of our top deck view.

CHAPTER 23

Boarhills to St Andrews

And finally the greatest sacrifice of all

WE WERE DRIVING towards East Neuk, the name for this coastal region of Fife. I sensed my heart beating and my breath quickening - my thoughts flitting from excited imaginings to quiet reflections in anticipation of my final walk ahead. The scenery sped by - the now familiar brow of the hill from Kinghorn to Kirkcaldy which I so loved, the sea front wall, the faster roads inland towards Leven and then the calming narrow roads of East Neuk. I was nearing my destination, nervous though inwardly pleased to walk this final stage on my own. My mind drifted.

'Are you sure this is the right way?' my husband asked as we zigzagged along minor roads across the countryside.

I looked down at the map and then up at the tiny single track ahead of us, meandering this way and that. An awkward moment and an endless minute passed until we arrived at the next junction. Realising my error I had to think quickly but in my confusion I sent us on another detour deeper into farmland. Occasionally I was reassured by a glimpse of the coast to our right. We can't be far away now I thought, crossing my fingers.

At the next junction I tried to sound more decisive.

'Turn right here and the first on your left and we'll be in the hamlet of Boarhills. Then we need to head out towards the coast where you can drop me off.'

Richard glanced sideways as if to be reassured, but my expression remained outwardly calm. We continued in silence. I couldn't put into words my need to complete this journey before we left Fife in May, and Richard couldn't understand the urgency. His week at work had been a tough one and so he had made the decision to drive on into St Andrews and meet me there, not having enough energy for what purported to be a 'challenging' section of the coastal trail.

'After all, we'll be back in a few months time,' he reasoned, to no avail. We agreed to differ. There was an uncomfortable atmosphere, only disturbed by the changing engine noises as Richard negotiated the tiny roads.

There were no goodbyes as he dropped me off at a coastal path signpost near a large barn in the middle of nowhere. I stood for a few moments, my coat, camera and small familiar rucksack at my feet - boots unlaced - and watched him drive off. Moments passed. I glanced at the deserted farmyard and absorbed my surroundings.

It was a glorious clear day. The sky was blue with the now familiar tinge of a yellowy white haze on the distant horizon. I breathed deeply. There was a slight breeze and for a moment I contemplated the superfluous layers of coat at my feet. A lone seagull squawked over-head, snapping me out of my reverie, flying purposefully down into the field nearby, as if watching me.

I let the day seep into me through my body to my finger tips and toes, bent to tie up my laces and put on my layers - just in case. Then I took another deep breath and strode along the straight path through the field towards the sea and the seagull. My husband now far from my mind.

Turning left at the cliff top I ambled along the hedge lined path, ever downwards until I reached the sandy grassy slopes above the beach. This certainly was not the challenging terrain I'd expected. I could keep up quite a pace, the evenness of my breath in rhythm with my steps. Occasionally I passed a rock adjacent to the path and wondered if they were ancient markers guiding the way for pilgrims over the centuries, especially in bad weather - fog perhaps. I paused to take a photo.

I've never felt totally alone throughout the nearly sixty miles of coastline covered so far, whether I have been on my own or with Richard. I've always been aware of other walkers - travellers following this holy trail throughout the ages. Today I felt their presence even more intensely. These shadowy hooded figures walked, always beside me and behind me - never in front. They appeared to have no desire to converse, just to keep me company. It was reassuring, as if they understood my vigil.

Soon I was climbing steps in the rock face, fit and full of energy by this time and invigorated by the sea air which filled me with a sense of well being. I was surprised, however, when the path evened out half way up the cliff - my shadowy friends falling in behind. Here the path, only a couple of feet wide, hugged the cliff face, only half way up the cliff, an unusual sensation. Though I'm often acrophobic I felt nothing but elation as I looked down to the rocky shore below and forward to the path I had no choice but to follow. There was no other way. At the next corner I paused and turned, looking behind me along the ragged empty coastline, savouring the anticipation as to what I would see around the bend. My companions seemed to dissolve into the rock-face as I gazed back. Sheltered from any sea breeze I took off my outer jacket and placed it in my rucksack as if unaware of the sheer drop beside me and the uncertainty which lay ahead.

In the quiet I could hear the trickle of water dripping down the cliff and a bee buzzing at my feet. My hands inadvertently rested on the rock beside me, the sun reflecting warmth and a salty earthy smell - small plantlets clinging to craggy nooks – details I might have missed had I been sharing this experience. The path was deserted and I revelled in my 'aloneness'.

Moving on I turned the corner, slightly saddened that my companions had deserted me for a while and within moments I heard a 'popping' sound above me, too crisp to be gunfire. I smiled as my overactive imagination sped through plots of murder and intrigue like a movie clip. 'Pop' the noise went again and I could hear voices over my head. I was closer to civilisation than I had imagined. I smiled, realising that the noise was a golf shot and above me must be one of the numerous courses surrounding St Andrews.

I glanced up at the sound of an engine, much like a lawn mower, in the direction of the open sea. A microlight aircraft had appeared and was flying in my direction. The man in the machine waved to me and then disappeared but a few minutes later came back as if to have another look at this lone female walker. I waved back this time but was glad when he vanished from view. The path climbed and followed the edge of the golf course for a while before dropping steeply to a cleft in the rocks - a wooden bridge spanned the stream between.

I was aware that my monk-like companions had returned, but instead of following me over the bridge they were striding the stepping stones below. I watched, mesmerised by their silent concentration as they avoided the worst of the running water, taking great care with each step.

The stream ran under me, a flow of water rushing down the rocks and then dispersing in the stony shoreline where it met the sea. I could almost taste its freshness before it mingled with the saltiness of the ocean.

I bent down to pick up a pebble and without too much thought I collected stones to make a small cairn, aware of my shadowy friends in an arc on the path behind me. With each stone I shed the burden of all that I had left behind in Bedfordshire - my home, my teaching career, family, friends, garden, business aspirations and dreams.

Although I knew that the seas would return and reclaim my pile of pebbles with the turn of the tide, dissolving it into the shore-line, I was reassured that my companions had witnessed my deed of *'letting go'*. I could leave my fate in their hands with the certainty that they would pray for me. It was tough to move on without one backward glance as I wondered if it was ever truly possible to leave a huge part of myself behind. 'Let go and let God,' people say. I thought of the razor shell I'd left with St Fillan and smiled - my sense of peace reflected in the rock pools nearby.

I focussed on each step as I took the path which climbed out of the cove and then descended quite steeply to a sandy inlet. Danger signs warned of high tides here, when the path would be impossible. I didn't pause for long - puzzled that the slippery rock face appeared to have no obviously visible signs of the path ahead. The sea was closer still. I could feel my heart beat and my shoulders tighten, nervous that I would be unable to find the way out.

Just as I was beginning to feel a glimmer of panic in the pit of my stomach, one of my companions passed me by. He placed his foot in what, a couple of seconds before, had been an invisible foothold, then he grabbed hold of the rocks above him and pulled himself up. Once safely above, he held out his hand. I felt a tingling sensation I can only describe as sheer joy as his fingers touched mine. His grasp was firm as I lifted my foot up to locate the tiny ledge in the rock-face. Once safely at the top I looked around to thank him but he had vanished, but I was sure he was part of the mass of shadows at the foot of the cliff. Waiting and watching.

The climb had brought me to a new level of rocky beach. Elated by the experience I rushed too fast and stumbled. My hands grazed on sharp rocks and I was aware of a throbbing pain in my right knee where I had tripped.

For a few moments I sat on a large rock, shaken by the experience and allowed a tiny shard of fear cut into me. What a silly place to be walking on your own! An inner voice rebuked. You are lucky your injuries are only minor ones, another more sensitive thought added.

I noticed an Auger shell in a crevice beside me - its sharply pointed spirals reminding me to trust in my own strength. Another sign.

Calm once more I could feel a presence over me, cutting out the sunlight. For the first time I saw the features of my companion's face, the one who had helped me earlier, and his deep grey eyes were smiling with a gentleness which encouraged me to get up. No real harm done, I thought, except maybe to my pride.

I smiled back at him as he gestured with a sweep of his arm and outstretched hand for me to continue on my way. Greatly reassured by his presence I walked on and ignored the throbbing pain of each step.

The path rose out of the bay and then descended once more and I was rewarded to be walking through an arch of pure white blossom. Delightful! I felt renewed and uplifted.

As the path opened out again to tufts of grassy stepping stones above the marshes I was quite disconcerted by the appearance of one cow - and then another. At first they were no real threat until I came across one who stood firmly in my way, astride the stepping stones which would take me safely across this wetland. I looked back but my companions showed no signs of guiding me at this point.

I walked gingerly towards the cow trying not to catch her attention or to look into her large round eyes. Talking quietly as I crept closer,

'It's Ok. I'm a friend,' I soothed. 'I'm not going to hurt you. I think you are a beautiful cow,' I added. I side stepped the cow on to the only free tuft of grass, to step past her. I was fearful that she would step backwards or, heaven forbid, lift her tail - a gesture which might have left me forever cleaning my boots. Nothing like that happened fortunately. She just glanced back at me and then continued to chomp on what must have been a truly delicious clump of grass.

Once over to the other side of this swampy ground I could caught a glimpse of my guardians who strode straight through the cow as if she didn't exist. Whether she felt the intrusion I'm not too sure, but she certainly lifted her head and made the loudest noise I'd heard since the microlight.

There was another steep climb ahead of me, all the more daunting with my knee in pain, but at least the steps were well made. Half way up I met the first fellow walkers of the day, obviously just out from St Andrews. At the top I was rewarded by a wonderful view of the city which shone in the sunshine - the ruined cathedral and the end of my journey deceptively close. I had glimpsed it on a couple of occasions during my walk, mirage-like in the misty haze but this was the first occasion I could pick out the features, and with the sun higher in the sky it looked stunning - a fitting place to end my pilgrimage.

I strode on. Soon my rugged path was replaced by tarmac and on the last hill down to the harbour a chill wind brushed my cheeks. Up until then the route I'd taken had been so sheltered and deceptively warm.

I paused to take a photo of the cathedral ruins and as I did so the path turned back into a dirt track and on the hill before me stood a magnificent cathedral, its spire, tower and surrounding turrets silhouetted on the skyline - a beacon of hope for seafarers and pilgrims alike.

I heard a cough behind me and turned to see a procession of monks back up along the path as far as my eyes could see, even on distant cliff tops. I took the hint to move on, followed by this throng. I reasoned from my previous reading that it must be in the 14th century and I wondered with anticipation as to what I was going to witness as we neared our destination. Not much further to go now.

On reaching the cathedral walls we were joined by a multitude walking from the city and as we merged into one mass of moving worshippers we drifted as one, ever closer towards our goal, a bee-like swarm homing in on their hive. We were not buzzing though – but in quiet contemplation and the only noise I heard was the shuffle of feet on stony ground, our bowed heads seeing only the sandals of the pilgrims in front. Our composure was shattered momentarily as we entered St Andrews Cathedral - all faces turned upwards in awe of its majesty. I shuffled with my companions. I was almost crushed to the wall of a side aisle with the three monks I recognised from their unwavering protection during my cliff top walk, just as a great hush fell over the throng.

I gazed silently through the vast pillars at the sea of people who filled every corner of the building. Suddenly the triumphal sound of the organ heralded the imminent arrival of a regal guest. The throng gasped in unison and strained their necks to see King Robert Bruce ride up the aisle on horseback for the proceedings to begin. A hush descended on the crowd in reverent respect as the king dedicated the cathedral to St Andrew.

I closed my eyes to join in the prayers but as I opened them I was aware of the light and the smell of sea air in the breeze once more. I stared around me, as much in awe of the ruins in which I now stood, as I had been of the Cathedral's interior moments before. An aura of holiness prevailed, emanating from the broken walls and arched windows, made magnificent still by the backdrop of the ocean. The pilgrims had vanished, replaced by tourists with cameras at every turn. I looked around me and in a shady corner I caught a glimpse of my three companions as they disappeared into the walls. The last monk, and my saviour on the rocks, turned once more and stared at me. Without a word spoken his message echoed around me like the sound of the sea below us,

'If you were asked to make the last and greatest sacrifice, what would it be?' - before he vanished. He did not smile but I could see deep into those penetrating grey eyes, which reminded me of someone, long after they had gone.

'Are you asking me to let go of my writing?' My whisper barely left my lips.

I stood for a while, my pilgrimage at an end. I had always planned to complete my journey here. I'd walked from The Forth Bridge at Queensferry -the place where St Margaret

142

once provided a route for travellers and pilgrims to cross the Forth, to St Andrews -a magnet for spirituality in the region.

Ode to St Andrews

On the hill top
majestic ruins enhance the blue skyline,
a backdrop for the restless ocean
and ribbon of white sands.
The cathedral's greatness
living on in the lives of countless pilgrims,
a memory of centuries of worship
and a legacy of spirituality.
A tribute to God.
And yet pilgrims also flock to the greens below,
the hallowed centre of golf.
Revered members
with their grand clubhouse
and fairways stretching
above the ocean and the endless sand.
A fitting tribute to the skills of man.

The Importance of St Andrews

There are many differing stories as to why the city bears the name of the Apostle St Andrew, mainly regarding relics of the saint which might have been brought there. The cathedral was built in 1158 being a magnet for pilgrims, but fell into ruin during the Scottish Reformation in the 16th Century. The university attracts students from all over the world. The pilgrims though, who flock to the St Andrews area in recent times are predominantly golfers and the city is said to be 'the home of golf.'

I have gained so much wisdom along the way but having arrived I am now standing still, aware that life is a series of paths, crossing and inter-crossing with those of others. Sometimes we will walk in parallel and at others following behind. Often, though, we need to be thankful to have times of solitude. There will be moments when we will have a heightened sense of awareness of those who have walked the same route years before us. Each path will be unique and we will continue to learn if only we keep an open mind.

Whilst standing amongst the cathedral ruins I was suddenly aware of the position of the sun high in the sky. I glanced at the time and texted Richard who agreed to meet me at the harbour. We drove in silence, both glad to get away from the crowds of St Andrews. I was unable to share my experience, apart from pleasantries about the walk. I did not fully understand it myself. Neither did I worry him about my fall and hid my limp over the next few days as my knee healed.

I was so deep in my own thoughts that I only remember glimpses of the drive back - snapshots of places on our walk along the coast and, as with any photograph, evoking a plethora of memories. Finally, we could see the estuary opening up in front of us and the clear view of the Forth Railway Bridge - magical in the light of early evening.

Reaching Pettycur felt so familiar – filled with the warm sensation of returning 'home.'

Epilogue

Back in Bedfordshire

MY DILEMMA AS to where to call 'home' is still as strong as ever, now that we have returned to Bedfordshire. We still look at properties for sale in Kinghorn on the internet and wonder what to do, but our debates go around in circles. After six months agonising over the decision we have made a peace with our lives here in Bedfordshire and put dreams to be beside the sea on hold for a while. There is a time for everything in life and nothing worthwhile should ever be forced. We will continue to visit and one day, maybe, we will know the time is right. I've taken the occasional photograph but no stranger has visited to impart their wisdom to me. Nevertheless, I am keenly aware of their presence in the shadows -John Bunyan is certainly close by.

As I look out of the window I see our garden coming to life for the spring, sheep ambling along the fence and the occasional woodpecker landing on the grass to peck - I didn't know they did that - and tiny finches flitting amongst the buddleia - but if I close my eyes ...

.....I can see the view out of the window at Pettycur as if it was in front of me - the changing sky and ever-moving sea. I can walk in my mind's eye down to the harbour where we spent many pleasant moments just dreaming and soaking up the smell of salt and seaweed. I can walk up Pettycur Road or make the climb up the cliff, panting for breath as I reach the top - pausing to admire the seascape before me. Taking a path through the houses I am excited to reach Doo Dells Lane. I love that name and have learnt since leaving that it stems from the colloquial word for male pigeons or doves - 'Doos' - who nest in the cliffs nearby, although we only saw seagulls there. It is our favourite path down to Kinghorn beach where seats are sheltered by the cliff face. My advice from experience though, is to take care to watch out for seagulls if you dare to take a picnic. Otherwise it is a perfect spot, secluded and unspoilt and, when the tide is in, this part of the bay is cut off from the main beach.

Our other frequent route is to amble along the Braes to the central path above the Lifeboat Station. I can skip in thought down the steps and admire the view out to the harbour. This time I'm going to creep past The Wee Shoppe and walk to the harbour's end where barely visible signs mark the direction of important landmarks - Edinburgh, Bass Rock and North Berwick and on this side of the Forth there's Kirkcaldy, Dysart, Buckhaven and far around to Earlsferry and the place my unseen companions joined me from their ferry from the south.

After a few minutes I am drawn back to the Wee Shoppe where the greeting is cheerful and the tea is good. You see, my imagination is nine-tenths reality. Maybe I am really there and only imagining being here in Bedfordshire. Now there's a thought!

PART 2

Letting Go and Moving On

CHAPTER 1

Revisiting East Neuk
and St Fillan

September 2016

WE WERE BACK in Fife enjoying a day out along the coast. I was standing beside Pittenweem harbour having spent a pleasant hour revisiting the village. It's my favourite place in East Neuk, a coastal region in the far south eastern corner of Fife, popular for its tiny unspoilt coves, bays and harbours. Pittenweem is not quite as jigsaw-puzzlesque as Crail, since it is still the working men's fishing harbour of the region, but in my opinion it is all the more lovely because of it. The smell of diesel mingles with that unmistakable fragrance of fish and seaweed. Each village has its own unique charm though. We bought some delicious artisan bread at the bakery and popped into The Cocoa Tree Cafe for a drinking chocolate. It is one of the many coffee shops in Pittenweem but we chose this one because, not only does it sell the most delicious orange drinking chocolate but it is from there that you can borrow the key to St Fillan's Cave.

After our refreshments Richard popped to the car to leave the bread for safe keeping while I returned to the cave, turning right at the church and down Cove Wynd towards the harbour. My hands were shaking as I opened the steel gate and found my way into its depths. I half expected to see my shells perching on the edge of the stone altar since my last visit. A volunteer must have tidied them away because it was spotless, no trace of shell or sand.

I stood wondering, pondering on all that had taken place since my last visit. So many changes in our lives. I stood in grateful silence trying to draw the seven shells from the depths of my memory.

An orange and brown *Trough* shell represented my *dream of being a writer* – well, my writing life had paused for nearly two years, but could this be the moment of rebirth?

My favourite pair of tiny purple and yellow *Branded Wedge* shells - oh yes, the most difficult to judge – my battle for *self worth* goes on.

A *Grey Top* shell for my gift of teaching. I am confident that I will find ways of using this gift in the fullness of time, but meanwhile I am involved in a community group who hope to re-open Kinghorn Library shortly and I am sure educational opportunities will arise in abundance.

A spiralling *Auger* shell reminding me to trust in my own strength and yet it has been learning to trust, but not necessarily in myself, which has enabled me to grow. A subtle difference.

A *Common Razor* whose name speaks for itself. I've let go of so much, some areas of my life more painful than others and I feel lighter somehow, as if I was carrying an enormous rucksack but I've left it behind.

Then there was the white *Common Cockle.* Yes, I can finally say that I am experiencing a balance between solitude to follow my own pursuits and self giving. More of that later.

Then, finally, the *Oyster* shell. Success in what? Life? All that I do? There were many proud times in my career as a teacher and the final moments, although a touch traumatic, were not of my own making. I certainly can't achieve further success as an author unless I take up the mantle again and work wholeheartedly towards my goal. I now have the time, space and drive to do so and the words of St Fillan echoed in my mind:

'It's not a sin to succeed Diana. You have pearl inside you. Believe in it.'

What was holding me back? Nothing!

I walked out of the cave, initially dazzled by the light and returned the key to the coffee shop before making my way down to the harbour to meet my husband. While I was waiting, soaking up the September sun as I gazed over the fishing boats, I was distracted by a small child who captured my attention as she flashed passed me. Within seconds she had slipped something out of her pocket and popped it into a nearby lobster pot creel before dashing back along the harbour to her family who were standing beside their car. Moments later there was an almighty din as her younger sister started yelling inconsolably. I watched as the wee tot was bundled into her car seat still crying. The picture of her tiny tearful face peering through the window was etched on my mind as the Fiat 500 pulled away. Memories of my own

Fiat 500, double declutching and the ability to park on a pavement made me smile momentarily.

Brought back to the present I glanced down at the harbour's edge and spotted a tiny doll, the size of a small child's hand in one of the creels. I looked up to see the car disappear from view. Had I been quicker, I thought, I could have retrieved the doll to return it to its rightful owner, thus saving all the tears? Too late. How many times do we ignore our instinct and miss opportunities? I vowed to be more aware in future.

At that moment my husband joined me and we began one of our favourite walks between Pittenweem and St Monans, admiring the unique floral bicycle displays as we left the village. At St Monans we were drawn to The Smokehouse, a cafe restaurant where you can eat right on the harbour's edge or over-looking the open sea towards the Isle of May.

'It's hard to believe that we are in east Scotland and not on the Mediterranean,' remarked my husband.

'It's not surprising that we love this part of the world,' I replied as we waited for our food, which turned out to be a delight.

Chapter 2

Where there's Life there's Hope

Late September 2016

A FEW WEEKS later we were out and about again visiting Culross, (pronounced *'Coorus'* I believe) a place steeped in historical charm. After we had climbed the cobbled streets of Tanhouse Brae and Kirk Street between the beautifully preserved and restored 16th century buildings to the Cistercian Abbey, we wandered through the monastery ruins.

I paused a while before climbing a blackened iron ladder; the remembered voices of St Mungo and St Serif echoing under the stone archway. I concentrated on their muffled words in the still shadows.

'Despite your misgivings, your life's journey has been relatively pain free, nevertheless, although I cannot offer you refuge I promise to watch over you as I did with Tenue all those ...,' then the words grew faint and I struggled to decipher their meaning. My eyes scanned the dark corners from whence the voice had come. There was silence. Reluctant to leave and unnerved by the sound of my own voice I whispered,

'I don't understand. Please don't leave me yet.'

I waited, then, just as I was about to turn away from the gloom and back into the sunlight, which glimmered through the trees, I think I heard,

'*Keep faith*,' as if a breeze blew softly in my ear. I stood still for a few moments longer before climbing back down to earth. Joining my husband in the ruins we ambled around before visiting the abbey. From the moment we entered the building there was a warm ambience which spoke of life, love, faith and community.

As I stood by the altar, the barely audible words, 'Keep faith,' left my lips.

'What did you say?'

'Nothing,' I paused. 'Isn't it peaceful in here?'

To me, a place of worship which has listened to believers over the centuries carries with it a certain presence, as if millions of prayers seep out of the very fabric of the church. Have you ever stood with the palms of your hands on ancient pillars, filled with awe of their majesty as if joined as one with people before you, from the stonemason to the present day? There are decorative roof bosses in Norwich Cathedral which tell that very tale. Awesome, if you'll forgive an expression corrupted by modern interpretations.

Retracing our walk, descending the steep slopes of Culross overlooking the Forth, we visited the Palace. Initially we turned to the cafe and gift shop spurred on by our excursions. I bought a local guide. Skimming through the notes on Culross Abbey and the village, my eyes were drawn towards the story of the unusual circumstances of St Mungo, whose story is entrenched in the history of the abbey, the original monastic site which was established by St Serif in the 6th century. The current Abbey was founded by The Earl of Fife in 1217, my guide book stated.

Teneu, the daughter of King Lleuddun of Gododdin, which we now know as the region of Lothian, was raped and unfortunately became pregnant. At that time, bringing a child into the world out of wedlock would bring such shame on the family that the penalty was death. The king ordered for Teneu to be thrown off Traprain Law in, what is now, East Lothian. It was a miracle that the princess survived the fall and so her injured body was left to the hands of fate and was placed in a coracle and set down on the Forth to drift with the tide. Luck shone down on Teneu that day since her boat beached further upriver at Culross. St Serif, the Abbot of Culross looked after her until the baby was born and named Teneu's child Mungo. Teneu and her child lived for many years in the safe confines of the abbey grounds.

At the age of twenty five years Mungo commenced his ministry by becoming a missionary and travelled to the region we now know as the City of Glasgow.

I smiled. In our days of long distance travel it is hard to imagine Glasgow needing a missionary. As we ambled around the Palace and its gardens, pausing occasionally in quiet contemplation, the story of Teneu merged in my mind with the little doll in the creel in Pittenweem, both stories of misplacement and separation. Teneu's tragic tale was replaced by springs of hope.

I pondered, reflecting on the changes in our own lives. You see, eighteen months after we left Fife we have returned, only this time permanently and we have spent the past ten months settling at home and getting involved in local community life. It is a truly remarkable place. Let me tell you briefly how it happened.

CHAPTER 3

Coincidence or God-Incidences

2014 to 2015

YEARS AGO I had a dear elderly friend whose name was Fred and his words, 'There are no coincidences in life, only God-incidences,' has remained with me ever since.

Our first year back in Bedfordshire was not easy. I don't think unplanned retirement ever is, especially when your loved one (me) is not ready to retire. Unable to concentrate on my own writing I threw myself into bringing my dream of a publishing cooperative into reality and I supported several local authors to bring their work to print. I also encouraged Richard to look for some pursuits in which to find fulfilment in his retirement. He spent the first few months catching up on neglected maintenance on the house, but also fretted about what he really wanted to do with his life. In truth he really didn't want to be there, and his frustration bubbled below the surface.

Suddenly, as the New Year of 2015 dawned he decided on a Gap Year - more a case of fulfilling his long held dreams. He planned various trips. We travelled to New York in February, to France in his Mark 2 Jaguar (which has sadly now been sold) in March and to Florida to visit the Space Station in May. On a personal note I bought into the whole space 'story' as we toured in awe of NASA's achievements, even the moon rock in the Apollo Centre, until, that is, I gazed up to see the Lunar Module, or in truth its replica.

"I just don't believe it,' I whispered to Richard. 'My primary children could have built it out of tin foil and cardboard. It looks so flimsy!'

Richard looked upon me with a frown, verging on disdain, not wishing any boyhood illusions to be questioned even for a moment, until he grinned,

'I know what you mean,' he said before we moved on.

I digress from my tale ... Latterly Richard volunteered at The Shuttleworth Collection which provided him with both enjoyment and a purpose for a while, until we reached his 61st birthday in June. Still not really settled into retirement in Bedfordshire and all the poorer financially after our adventures, we acknowledged that something was missing in our lives. Inadvertently we started to look towards Scotland once more, a place where we had both been so happy.

We had visited Fife several times in the past year to catch up with friends, so we were not surprised when I had a text message,

'There's a flat for sale in Pettycur a couple of doors away. Interested?'

Richard checked on the website and liked the look of it and so he booked a cheap flight north for the day, to view the place.

It was not meant to be. Everything seemed to be put in our way, including a change in the closing date for bids, making it impossible for us to alter our travel arrangements in time without incurring huge costs. Meanwhile Richard was browsing properties on the Internet and saw a house which caught his attention.

'We have our tickets booked so why not give it a look over?' he said and so we arranged an appointment. We flew up and were surprised that the lady who came to the door recognised me.

'We were only talking about you and Richard at the Kinghorn in Bloom meeting last night,' she said, 'and we wondered if you were the couple who were flying from down south to view my house today.'

Although I was the one who was initially sceptical about the idea of a permanent move to Fife, away from close family and friends, I fell in love with the house straight away. It was perfect for us. Later, when my husband had second thoughts, I remained firm. '*Keep Faith*,' echoed in my ears. I was sure that it was the right time for us. The downstairs was a great place for guests or even for a granny annexe if the need arose. It had a lovely, albeit quite small terraced cliff face garden, which would certainly be a new challenge for me and the house was perfectly located half way between Pettycur and the Royal Burgh of Kinghorn, as it is now known officially.

CHAPTER 4

Moving in

December 2015

FIVE MONTHS LATER, after a nail biting sale of homes, each cherished with a hope that the new owners would continue to love them, we were heading north once more, only this time it was for real.

'You realise that they've closed The Forth Bridge to keep you out,' friends joked as we prepared for the long journey, having already sent all our worldly goods northwards.
(The road bridge was closed for emergency repairs)

We'd had an enormous de-clutter. Our life in Fife was to be simpler; a smaller more manageable garden, buying locally where we could, walking rather than using the car and finding our place in community life.

Within moments of moving in, neighbours had welcomed us and invited us in for tea. As we awaited the arrival of our furniture, delayed by the bridge closure with estimated arrival unknown, we looked around the house and then stood in the lounge gazing across the water towards Edinburgh. Excited, albeit a little nervous about the future we stood side by side. Waiting, enjoying the quiet.

My only frustration was that I had planned to launch *'From Redundancy to Rejuvenation'*, part one of this story, in

Kinghorn that November but God had other ideas. We moved here a month too late. I was frustrated at every turn. After a few lapses of confidence I let this one go too. Having little time to promote it, the book drifted to the back of my mind. I gave the occasional copy away and the response was overwhelming. Many people who read it loved it but something was holding me back. Was it the monk's prophesy coming true? Did I know instinctively after my walk along the coastal path to St Andrews that I would need to leave behind my passion for writing? Would that change once I was fully involved in life here in Fife? I had no answers, only more questions.

Over Christmas and New Year we renewed friendships and became acquainted with our neighbours, who have now become special friends. Two trips down south, either side of the festive season were a little unsettling, but we had boxes to unpack and belongings to sort. We had moments of frustration too, when we couldn't find things. Everyone does. One great loss was that my old camera was missing, and now, a year on, we still have not unearthed it. It's possible that it's in one of the unpacked boxes at the back of the garage or it may have, inadvertently, gone to a charity shop down south amongst the so many 'no longer needed by us' items. If it has, then I can only pray that the next owner enjoys its quirky magic as much as I did.

This reminded me of the saying that everything is on loan to us. We own nothing and, since we cannot take a single treasure with us beyond our mortal journey, we need to appreciate our gifts fully while we have the chance.

The festive season was not the best of times to get involved, but a time for ourselves to enjoy our new surroundings. One night Richard encapsulated our feelings,

'I'm sure we were brought here for a reason. The hardest thing is being patient and waiting to find out what that reason is.'

Very soon we began our involvement in Kinghorn life. Not a difficult task in such a thriving and active community. I was reflecting on this one day when I went for a walk on my own. I summed our new life quite succinctly in my diary :

17th April 2016

'Today I donned my wellington boots, walked down to Pettycur Harbour and out to the place where the ripples in the sand greet the gentle lapping of the waves. As I often do on moments such as this I thought of my elderly friend Fred who taught me how to pray for people on each wave. Beginning with family and then friends, both down south and newly formed here in Fife, I silently spoke their names into the wind as each wave lapped over my boots.

I mentioned each of my family and close friends, both old and new, including the cheerful group of Kinghorn in Bloom, with their visions to enhance the beauty of the village, even if it meant picking up cigarette ends. Next I named the folks we meet at The Wee Shoppe and at The Crown for a blether. Finally I thought of each member of the dedicated bunch in Kinghorn Library Renewed who hope to be running a Kinghorn community library when, sadly, The Fife Cultural

Trust library closed its library doors at the end of February 2017.

Each name hovered silently on my lips and in my head and I was thankful. I was comforted with the notion that the waves continued their prayers long after I had left the beach.'

7th May 2016

'Six months on and I realise today that we have never been happier in all of our married lives. Richard has shed the stress of life and work down in Bedfordshire. Even when things don't go quite right the sight of the sea soothes us, and we have a good laugh. We've never laughed so much together. It has certainly enriched our marriage.'

Moving north hasn't avoided all the usual frustrations and mishaps in life, but we are learning to handle them with good grace. One of our local minister's sermons has remained in my mind. He spoke of King Solomon who, when he was to become King over Israel, prayed to be wise and to have an understanding heart, rather than for riches, good health or even peace. Wise words from a wise King!'

CHAPTER 5

A Short Personal Dip into Darkness

Early September 2016

WE ENJOYED A plethora of activity throughout the summer with plenty of visitors interspersed with trips down south. Our time here was full too, helping out with Kinghorn in Bloom as they prepared for the judging for Beautiful Fife and Beautiful Scotland. Then there was The Village Show, where competition to win a first prize is serious but also causes hilarity. Fancy doilies will certainly not be allowed under the cakes or scones next year!

After such an intense period of busyness I admit to feeling an occasional gnawing of unease and emptiness that I was uncertain how to fill. It was my turn for my frustrations to surface and I prayed desperately for an answer. Had I taken on too much? Was my brain coping with such a life changing experience? Was I too young to retire or should I look for a 'real' job?

One day, when I really wanted to lose myself in gardening, Richard suggested that we fulfil one on our *'to-do-list'* and drive to Queensferry to walk over the Forth Road Bridge. It was a sunny Saturday in September, a short T-shirt sort of a day, that pleasant ambient temperature which I so love about this region of the UK. We took our fleecy jackets, thinking it might be windy 150 feet above the Forth, but we didn't need them. Saturday is the best day to do this walk because both pathways, either side of the road, are open to walkers and cyclists. Taking the path from North Queensferry and up the steps on to the bridge we soon felt invigorated. It took a few moments to become accustomed to the traffic thundering to our right, but soon I relaxed, knowing that the barriers were there to protect us.

First we walked over the east side, the village of North Queensferry below us. A stunning view of The Forth Rail Bridge was to our left through which we caught glimpses of the Fife Coast, a region we had come to know and love. My demeanour was soon uplifted. As we reached the central point, before we began our descent, we paused a while. Gazing further out we could see Pettycur in the misty sunshine and beyond it to the North Sea. Looking upwards the towering structure appeared so firm and unyielding and yet I knew that faults lay hidden beneath. I had a fleeting thought. Was this a mirror of my life? Why had the Forth Rail Bridge, so solidly orange and unwavering, lasted over 125 years? What a Victorian feature of engineering to marvel at!

We continued our walk until the waters of the Forth were no longer below us but the cobbled street of the historic village of South Queensferry. This meandered towards the foot of the rail bridge. Should we pause and walk down to the village for a coffee, or press on?

We decided to take the underpass and complete our walk before searching for refreshments, emerging on the west side with a completely different view of the Forth. Immediately in front of us was The Queensferry Crossing, the new Forth road bridge, almost complete. I'm told that state of the art electronic sensors, to ensure that it is structurally sound and safe, are woven into its infrastructure. I was speechless for a moment and transported in my mind back to my meeting with John Fowler more than two years previously. I remembered his words as I grappled with the present.

'So why are you dithering? Why do you waste so much time? Write, write, write and with each word improve your skills.'

So why **was** I dithering?

The return walk seemed quicker. I thought of our recent trip in a tour boat along the Forth to Inchcolm Island. It had been an unexpectedly sunny and warm April day and as we had cruised under the three bridges we were mesmerised as a missing piece of the new structure paused on a barge close by, like an unfinished jigsaw. As writers and probably artists do too, my imagination was on overdrive as I saw the large arm of God lifting the piece into place. Today, with only two pieces to go, it was uncanny how my mind's eye saw the beauty of the whole, rather than focussing on the gaps; the white fluorescent towers proudly holding their cables aloft, reminded me of the curve stitching of my childhood. We paused to look at the new aircraft carrier *HMS Queen Elizabeth,* being completed in Rosyth, before leaving the bridge and walking back down to North Queensferry, taking a footpath closer to the river before pausing in one of our favourite bistro cafes.

'I'm sorry but we don't have a table,' said the waitress.

'That's Ok,' I said. 'Let's go to The Albert Hotel,' I turned to Richard. 'It seems right somehow to finish our walk there.'

I confess that this was our first actual visit. We sat on a corner table with the window looking out towards Fife's most famous burnt orange icon, the Forth Rail Bridge. The hotel bar was just as I had imagined it. A sudden thought occurred to me that would make true historians nod and say *I told you so*. I was hit by the question, was The Albert Hotel in existence when the first bridge was being built? I try to research thoroughly but, in that moment, I frowned at my own shortcomings, my insecurities returning. Later that night I searched it on Google. What a relief! Queen Victoria and Prince Albert alighted at North Queensferry in 1842, after which the hotel was given its name, nearly fifty years before the bridge was completed.

Back at home Richard looked thoughtful. Realising that I was still struggling with each day, when he was on top of the world, high on activities and life in Fife, Richard was nevertheless extremely supportive. He was concerned in the change in my demeanour.

'What do you think the problem is?' he asked me, his eyes full of concern when a small thing had become huge in my eyes and I was acting as if I was suffering from the most painful women's problems!

'I'm not sure. I really don't know,' I sighed, retreating to the patio for a moment of peace and quiet reflection.

Recently a couple of authors had expressed their desire for me to take up the mantle of publishing again. Was it time?

Also, as I was weeding the Braes alongside a new recruit from Kinghorn in Bloom, the lady remarked,

'I've read your book and it's lovely, especially the parts about Pettycur. There's a message in it isn't there? My only thought is that it's obviously not the end of your story. When are you going to share what happened next?'

My mind drifted with the various shades of grey cloud, briefly obscuring the sunshine.

I was confused. Had I really left my writing life far behind me? Had I truly *let go*? Or was it waiting in the wings for the right cue.

CHAPTER 6

A Gannet Meditation

I PAUSED IN my reflections a while to absorb the September sunshine now breaking through over the Forth towards Edinburgh. My eyes were drawn to a small colony of gannets sitting on rocks just off the shoreline. The tide was turning, creeping slowly in over the sand flats. I was inexplicably filled with empathy for these birds. A group on the periphery took flight, attracting my closer scrutiny. I ran down the wooden steps and through to the lounge to pick up a pair of binoculars.

Don't ask, my eyes implored my quizzical husband as I fled back outside. As I watched through the lenses I almost held my breath, mesmerised as one of the flock flapped its wings in that ungainly fashion so typical of gannets, wings pointing downwards. To my surprise he settled down again on the rock as if waiting for the right moment. A bird, already swimming in the water nearby took flight, his wings skimming the sea. I was so mesmerised by this graceful departure that I nearly missed the sight of a wave which washed the claws of another bird knocking her off balance. She steadied herself with the span of her wings and stubbornly remained, gripping to the rock.

Whilst watching the sea at the turn of the tide, seconds like this can seem an hour and each hour a lifetime. It was in these moments of gannet reflection, when time seemed to stand still, that I remembered my shells. I longed to find true meaning in my life but, like the gannets, was I still clinging to areas of my life or did they still have power over me? Beneath the calm I was impatient to be free of all that was holding me back.

What will these birds do when the rocks are finally submerged? I wondered. Will all of the gannets take flight? Only four remained. A white surge of water washed one bird into the sea and within a few moments it was gliding with its wing tip just above the waves to join the flock, and then another until only two remained on the largest of the rocks, still visible above the surface. When the sea finally covered their refuge, these last two defenders began swimming in the water, circling the almost submerged rocks as if unwilling to let go. Familiarity, supremacy, or just energy conservation? I wondered what force was making them cling on to a safety that was no longer there.

All that now remained was a whirlpool of flickering light, a sign of the rocks beneath, as this pair circled once more before finally flying away.

Finally it was time to 'let go' of my perceived reality; one that no longer existed. I breathed in deeply and let my breath out very slowly, to dissipate in the crisp morning air. It was at that moment that I experienced a sense of freedom to pursue my personal destiny; a freedom to revive my business, or at least to seek a greater clarity as to its intended direction, and yes, finally I felt free to write again.

I went back inside and made a cup of tea, that panacea of all things good in British life, certainly in mine anyway.

'Thanks. You look happier, 'Richard looked questioningly into my eyes.

'I think I know what the problem was.' I paused to smile. 'I think I've been so concerned that we should settle down and enjoy a fulfilled life here that I've lost some important parts of myself along the way - especially my need to be creative and to write.'

'There's nothing stopping you now,' Richard replied. 'Go for it!' and he stood up and we hugged. To go forward with Richard's blessing had truly set me free. On that day the essence of Part two of this 'memoir', *Letting Go and Moving On*,' was born.

CHAPTER 7

A Moses Moment

Back to Culross in Late September 2016

AFTER LEAVING CULROSS Palace, with its distinct burnt orange rendered walls, we were standing in Culross Square, a place so photogenic that if you search for it on Google Images a plethora of virtually identical but equally stunning shots roll out. As we took the path at the water's edge back to the car I turned for a moment and looked east towards Rosyth. Pictures of Teneu's journey filled my imagination.

I like to call this my *Moses Moment* because, in that instant, thoughts became words and phrases became sentences which tumbled out of my head. You see, though I've always had a passion to write, nearly two years ago I let go of that creative element of my psyche to allow space in my life for other opportunities for the greater good. It was as if my gift with words - a phrase used by others and not myself, had been buried deep inside me, but was still alive and waiting for that moment to be reborn. My fingers were ready to fly over the keys again!

October 6th 2016
I wrote in my diary:

'The recent clouds in my brain lifted from dark grey to white and then today, the sun has returned to every corner of my life and the keyboard is tapping once more. I have several unfinished projects, but my priority is to finish the second part of this book.'

November 1st 2016

Richard has joined the local Rotarians and we have both been helping at the Pop Up Charity Shop for the last few days. Today was our first clear day and Richard thought I would want to get back to my writing, but it was such a lovely day.

'Why don't we walk up The Binn Hill?' I suggested over breakfast. 'We've always wanted to do that and it's such a clear day.'

Richard agreed and so we set off to park at Kinghorn Loch, with just a couple of bottles of water. The paths above Craigencalt Farm are well kept and we waved to a chap we knew who was working on his allotment.

'How long do you think it'll take us to reach the top?' I asked.

'Oh, about half an hour or so,' he answered, so we set off at a pace, enjoying the winter sunshine, initially taking us through the woodlands above the Loch. Next the route dipped down to the road which we followed for a few yards before taking a path to our right, through a gate and passing a standing stone, probably recently positioned.

The walk was gentle at first and we paused to read the information boards on the shale oil industry which began in the area over 100 years ago. Nothing is new is it? We had heard of the abandoned village up here but never absorbed the history until now.

The last two sections of the path were quite steep, all the more slippery since it had rained heavily the night before. I made a mental note to remember not to be fooled by a beautiful clear winter's day in future and to keep to rambles at a lower altitude. If it were icy it would not be a wise route to walk. Anyway, with drainage fairly good, we were able to reach the top safely and, wow, it was worth the effort.

From here we could see as far as The Forth Bridge to the west, with the road bridge and the New Queensferry Crossing behind. Burntisland was below us and Arthur's Seat and Edinburgh Castle were visible over the water.

My eyes swept along the south bank of the Forth all the way to Bass Rock and North Berwick. Teneu and her perilous journey all the way to Culross came to mind. I peered further west but no, the Cistercian Abbey of Culross was not visible from where we were standing, but I could imagine it in the far distance. I allowed my eyes to scan slowly along the northern shore of the river, and I caught a glimpse of the tip of Pettycur Harbour. Further on the three towers of Kirkcaldy led my eyes towards Dysart, Wemyss and finally to Earlsferry before the coast vanished north eastward, towards Elie and on to St Andrews. My vivid imagination was transported for a second to the top of the cliff following my chain-link walk challenge. The distance I'd travelled physically, emotionally and spiritually lay before me.

I sighed and was brought back to the moment.

'It's so beautiful!' I smiled at Richard.' We are so lucky to live here.'

He reached out for my hand smiling back. I'd arrived at last. We sat on the bench for a wee while in companionable silence absorbing the view, the fresh air and the winter sunshine.

'Maybe we'd better head back down again. We've a dental appointment at 3 pm,' Richard's down to earth comment broke though the breezeless calm. I grinned. You really have moved house when you visit a new dentist.

'Come on then, slowly does it though. We don't want to fall and break any teeth!'

Just before the descent I glanced over my shoulder to the north and the Lomond Hills. Maybe, they'll be the next challenge, I thought, but best wait 'til the spring.

Today, December 7th, is exactly a year since we moved to Scotland and I noticed a joyful news item in the Fife Free Press which made my heart soar with thankfulness.

Tina's doll saved from the jaws of a Forth Lobster

Tina, a five year old from Kirkcaldy was reunited with her favourite doll, lost at Pittenweem six months ago. Like Jonah and the whale, fisherman Andy was surprised to find the doll in the mouth of a lobster, recently caught in The Firth of Forth. His catch, along with the doll, travelled in the fish van along the south coast of Fife, visiting towns and villages en-route. Can you imagine the delight on Tina's face when her mum, who sometimes bought fish for the family at Andy's van, recognised the doll in his windscreen. The fish man was delighted to reunite Tina with her favourite doll.

'What a catch!' they said.

Afterwards, Thanks and an Apology

WRITING THIS JOURNAL has been a pleasure and cathartic too. I have enjoyed researching into the history of our adoptive home of Fife immensely, but the journey has also been a way of letting go - a path of healing and of understanding my priorities in life. Above all it has been a way of showing my gratitude to the community of Fife for their welcome and for opening our eyes to their beautiful Coastal Path.

I have tried to update this edition to reflect any changes since 2013 especially in cafés open, but times move on and businesses thrive or go under so forgive me if you find that I speak of places no longer in existence or occasions no longer celebrated. I believe that The Coastal Path Challenge has now replaced The Spooky Walk in aid of the RNLI for example, but by the time you read this it might have reverted back again!

I have so many people to thank. First of all thanks to my husband, who shares this life with me, but who is never quite sure whether I'm really somewhere else! Heartfelt thanks to Alex and Moira and the family of friends we made at the Wee Shoppe - in fact to all those who made our initial stay in Pettycur and Kinghorn a delight. More recently thanks to all of those who have welcomed us as neighbours and as part of the community of Kinghorn, where we now feel so at home.

I am indebted to my editors Brenda and Marcus Webb, to Sue Ayres, Elizabeth Whitton and Pam Henderson for their valuable proof reading and feedback and to the community of authors at Eventispress for their genuine encouragement.

To finish with an apology - Any mistakes are all mine, especially in trying to capture the Scottish lilt. I can imagine as I write, people having a wee blether about the book and saying,

'Och, d'ya ken this. We dunna speak like that. Diana's got it all wrong, bless her!'

Although my personal pilgrimage has come to an end, The Fife Coastal Path winds on to Dundee, and if you are continuing that way, although I will not be with you, I'd love you to share your experiences with me. Maybe you have met different significant strangers in your path and have had equally special adventures. I'd love you to get in touch and share your experiences with me. You can reach me in many ways:

email diana@dianamaryjackson.co.uk
tweet me @Riduna
visit my Diana Jackson's author page on Facebook
or visit one of my blogs -
www.selectionsofreflections.wordpress.com
www.dianamj.wordpress.com
I'd be delighted to hear from you.

The Fife Coastal Path

If you would like to walk along the Fife Coastal Path please can I encourage you to buy:

'*Fife Coastal Path - footprint*' - a map with lots of important information, including high tide routes, the difficulty of the paths, car parks, refreshment stops and toilets. It has a useful waterproof holder.

'*The Fife Coastal Path - The Official Guide*' An excellent resource book including maps, tourist information and detailed descriptions of the walks by official rangers noting landmarks, flora and fauna and a wealth of fascinating facts.

There is now an official *Fife Pilgrim's Way*, from Culross to St Andrews, or starting at North Queensferry as we did. It is a 70 mile walk, of which we probably covered about 60 miles.

My maps included in this book were drawn 'free hand' using '*Paint*'. They are only very rough - the lumps and bumps are as likely to be a slight of hand rather than accurate contours of the coastline but they do give you an impression as to where places are in relation to each other.

The real maps and books above can be bought in many locations along the way including tourist information, bookshops and resource centres, for example the lovely Harbourmaster's Cafe at Dysart or on the Internet.

Other Books by Diana Jackson

Riduna (historical saga set on the island of Alderney 1865 - 1910)

Ancasta Guide me Swiftly Home (second in The Riduna Series set in Southampton and The Channel Islands 1910 - 1920)

The Life and Demise of Norman Campbell (a memoir of a 103 year old who went to Australia in the 1920's, returned and saw both world wars, lived a full life and became a silver surfer at 102! 1909 - 2012)

Murder, Now and Then (Two murders in Bedfordshire ~ 100 years apart ~ 1919 and 2019)

110

Printed in Great Britain
by Amazon

45243238R00106